LIVING IN
SAVAGE TIMES

BY
RONNIE BURKE

ISBN
Hardcover: 978-1-967668-03-8
Paperback: 978-1-967668-04-5

Foreword

The title of this book came from a line used in a sermon I heard on a podcast. I cannot remember the title of the sermon or the name of the speaker, but that statement stuck in my mind. Since that time, I came to a deep agreement that the speaker was right. We are living in Savage times.

These times are a threat to the family, marriage, children, the church, and others in our society. I never thought I would live through a time when men and women determined that they were the wrong gender. I never thought I would see boys playing against girls in sports or the boys would enter a boxing match with girls. These events are bad enough, but what is worse they are being promoted and supported by political and even religious leaders.

However, the conclusion of all of these disturbing trends is that God is on the throne. He is not surprised by these challenges. He is not wringing His hands, wondering where everything went wrong. No, He is in control.

Since we serve a God who loves us and is in control of all things, we can rest and be at ease because this God who has everything under control is the God who loves us.

Acknowledgments

Special thanks to my friend and fellow minister, Mike Rodrigue who was my reader and critic, offering valuable suggestions to make the book more readable and relatable to those who chose to read it.

Special thanks and gratitude to my granddaughter Anna Currie, who designed the cover art.

Contents

Chapter 1: We Are Here For A Purpose

These past three years have been very difficult and sad. First, we lived through a worldwide pandemic. Hundreds of thousands of people around the world died from the COVID-19 virus. We witnessed men and women going to the hospital and never leaving. They died without family members present because of the health protocols. Doctors and nurses who worked with these patients also experienced illness and sometimes death.

It was during that time the church was able to remind the world that we are never alone. We are always in the presence of Jesus. He promised that He would never leave us or forsake us at any time. We had the opportunity to share the wonderful message of the presence of Jesus, no matter where we are or what circumstances we find ourselves in.

However, this is only one example of the savage times we are living in. I am going to talk about some of these difficult times and events. As difficult as these times are, I want to remind the reader that we serve a God who has the answer to everything traumatic we are experiencing. Those of us who are believers have His presence in and around us. We have His wisdom and peace indwelling us. We enjoy His guidance when we are not sure where to go or what to do.

The other thing that is good to know is that the God we serve is not flustered or confused about what to do during these times. He is not in heaven worried about what to do. He is in control of all things. Not only that, but He lives in us and wants us to be the voice of hope for a hurting world.

In the following chapters, we will discuss some of these savage events, such as

1. The continued fight over abortion.

2. The savage abuse of children going through transgender indoctrination and, sometimes, brutal and life-changing surgery.

3. The rise of antisemitism on our college campuses.

4. The violence against police officers.

5. District Attorneys in some cities are unwilling to enforce laws against criminals.

6. The failed immigration policies.

7. Understanding what the greatest threat to Democracy is.

8. The promotion of CRT (Critical Race Theory)

9. The lies of DEI. (Diversity, equity, and inclusion)

10. The war in the Middle East between Israel and Hamas.

11. The war in Ukraine.

These are just some of the problems we faced. All of these challenges show us how limited we are in being able to do anything about them. But there is good news. We have a God who not only is able to solve all of these problems but can also help us navigate through these troublesome times.

God put us here in this time because, as always, we, the church, the people of God, are the only ones who have the answers people are looking for today. We are the only people who can bring about real and lasting change in the hearts of men and women, not through our own power and strength but through the power of God, who works through us. We are here to give hope to those who are hopeless. We are here to point men and women to the only person who can give them what they need and satisfy every longing in their hearts.

The church was born in the midst of oppression and hopelessness.

On the day of Pentecost, the church was born. It was born in a time of religious and political oppression. It was born during a time when men and women from all over the world needed answers to their spiritual problems. On the day of the birth of the church, Peter stood up and spoke to the crowd of people there. His sermon had one goal and that was to point to Jesus. He wanted that crowd to know that Jesus was the answer for their life. He said:

"Men of Israel, hear these words: Jesus of Nazareth, a man attested by God to you by miracles, wonders and signs which God did through Him in your midst. Him you have taken by lawless hands, have crucified and put to death, who God raised up, having loosed the pains of death."

-(Acts 2:22-24 ESV)

The great message of the gospel is that Jesus is alive. This does not mean that He rose from the dead, ascended into heaven, and sat passively on the throne. No, we serve a Lord who not only knows all that is going on, but He is a God who is actively involved in our lives.

The God who showed up on the day of Pentecost is the God who has been showing up all through history.

"God showed up in a burning bush to call Moses to lead Israel out of Egypt."

-(Exodus 3:1-15. ESV)

"God showed up at the Red Sea to create a path for the Jews to walk through to the other side."

-(Exodus 14)

"God showed up in the fiery furnace with the three Hebrew Children. When they were thrown into the fire, the King looked and saw not three but four men in the fire. He said that the fourth man's face looked like the son of God."

-(Daniel 3:21-25. ESV)

"God showed up in the lion's den with Daniel."

-(Daniel 6:16-22 ESV)

"God showed up in Bethlehem in the form of a baby."

-(Luke 2 ESV)

"God showed up on Calvary to save us from our sins."

-(Matthew 27 ESV)

In these times, we must remember that God is still showing up.

One of my favorite movies is FOREST GUMP. Forest is a simple man but has tremendous insight in spite of his handicaps. In the movie, Forest buys a shrimp boat and names it "Jenny" after the woman he loves. His former lieutenant from Vietnam joins him on his boat to help him in the shrimping business. However, Lt. Dan is very angry and upset that he was rescued in Vietnam. Lt Dan always had the impression that it was his destiny to die in battle like previous members of his family.

In one scene, Forest and Lt. Dan are in the middle of the ocean looking for shrimp. Lt. Dan is on the mast of the ship, raging at God for not letting him die in Vietnam. In one statement, he challenged God to show Himself. He wanted to face God and complain about how unfairly he had been treated.

As the scene continued, the winds began to build and grow more fierce. Forest's comment was epic. He said, "And God showed up." The scene continues, and they struggle through the storm. After the storm subsides and they survive, Lt. Dan appears to be at peace. Forest observes, "I guess Lt Dan finally made peace with God." (FOREST GUMP; THE MOVIE, Released 1994)

I love that line; "God showed up." The reason I love that line is because it speaks a very true statement of God's interaction with His church throughout history. We could look at many historical moments and see the hand of God working in the lives of others. However, I want us to see how God shows up today. I want us to see examples of the hand of God moving and working in the midst of our own cultural, political, and social chaos.

God is aware of what each of us is going through. He knows about the pains, struggles, persecutions, and hostility we face. Because He knows all of the details of our lives, He is able to give us what we need in difficult moments. Not only is He aware of what we are going through and what troubles us, but He also hears us when we pray. He hears us when we are hurting or troubled because of events happening around us and to us. Don't ever lose heart, dear friend; God loves you, hears you, and is continually with you. YOU ARE NOT ALONE,

Most of the events of recent times are because people want change. A lot of suggestions are made about the changes needed, but sadly the changes that took place were mostly shallow and insignificant. For instance:

The pancake mix named Aunt Jemima was changed because it was considered racially charged. But when you open the box with the new name, you are going to get the same thing you always got: pancake mix. Only the name is changed.

Mrs. Butterworth's syrup is still a syrup.

Eskimo pie is still an ice cream sandwich.

Uncle Ben's rice is still rice. Changing the name of a product does not change the product.

But when Jesus changes us, we are not the same.

We were spiritually dead; now we are alive.

We were blind, but now we see

We were lost, but now we are found.

We were sinners doomed for hell, but now we are saints on our way to heaven.

We are a new creature in Christ. Everything about us is different.

Jesus made this change in us so we could change the world.

As I stated at the beginning, those who are believers in Christ are here to make a difference in our world. When the church was born on the day of Pentecost, the world was under the control of Rome. The Roman government could be ruthless in the way it enforced its laws. Most of the world at the time was enslaved. Many people lived on the edge of starvation. Most would work for a day's wage to buy just enough food to sustain themselves. There were days of violent revolt against the government. There were zealots who had one desire, and that was to overthrow the Roman government and make Israel a free state. It was this kind of world the church was born in.

The church has always lived in turbulent times. There are very few times in history where there was relative peace and prosperity. Many government leaders were corrupt and persecuted the church. Even the established church, through the years, persecuted those who did not follow the prescribed doctrines. People lived in a state of hopelessness. Most felt that they could never become any better off than they were at the moment.

Through the years, the world has experienced wars and revolutions. The church was in the midst of those moments providing the message of hope.

In some places, it is illegal to become a Christian. In the Middle East, Christians are hunted down and persecuted. The leaders of house churches are thrown in jail. Some of them are executed for blasphemy against the Prophet Mohammed.

Today, even in our free society, the church is experiencing a certain level of persecution and hostility. We will talk about many of those things in the coming chapters.

I wanted us to understand that God put us here during these times with the same purpose he put other Christians living in former times. He put us here to be the salt and the light for the world. He put us here to give the message of hope to those who are hopeless. He put us here to express and live out the joy that comes with knowing Him. He put us here to be an example in marriage and in parenting. He put us here to be an example of doing the best work possible on the job we have. He put us here to speak for Him and let everyone around us know He offers eternal life for everyone who asks.

If we are going to be effective in fulfilling our purpose for being here, then we must examine our own Christian Walk. We need to answer some questions concerning where we are spiritually.

How is our prayer life? What do we pray for? I believe that one of the problems for the church is that we undervalue prayer. It seems that many churches spend a lot of energy and effort on programs and activities. They have activities for every age group and every season and, for the most part, can get a large number of people to attend. We need to be reminded that prayer is the greatest activity we can do. Prayer is calling on the power of God to do what we cannot do.

How is our Bible Study life? How much do we read and study each day? How much do we meditate on this word? The more we put this word in our hearts, the more that we are going to have the ability to reach the world for Christ. How much are we seeking the face of God? To really seek the face of a god means that we cannot be satisfied with just a devotional reading of scripture before we go to bed. We cannot be satisfied with just a casual prayer.

What is our passion for the Lost? How much do we want to see men and women saved? As we watch the violent protest taking place, we see a lot of passion and energy. What kind of passion for Christ are we living out in our lives?

How strong is our passion to make a change or a difference in our culture? I know that we are seeing some disturbing things, but do we have the passion to find a way to make a difference around us.

The attitude of the world towards the church is that it is irrelevant. Many don't believe the church has any value in the world. They consider the church to be outdated and irrelevant. But we are not irrelevant. The church is the most vital institution created by God. The church is the body of Christ living out His love and grace to the world. The church has the only message of how to have a relationship with God that is eternal.

We are to live in a way that reveals just how relevant the church is to the world. We can go out every day on our jobs, our communities, and our schools and reveal the relevance and beauty of the church through the kind of life we live. We can show the glory of Jesus by how we reveal the joy in our hearts, the kindness in our voices, and the love we express to others. We can reveal the relevance of the church by letting Jesus live His life through us.

Finally, we must remember who we are. We are to live in such a way that reveals our identity as Christians. I mentioned earlier that one of the problems facing our culture today is the misunderstanding of gender. Some adults and young people identify as a gender that contradicts their own biology. Some men identify as women. Some women identify as a man. This confusion caused some to go through radical surgeries to change their physical features. Radical surgeries are being performed on young children. Ever since the question of gender arose, more and more gender identities do not have the emotional or intellectual capacity to understand the idea of gender.

The social culture now has determined there are more than two genders. Depending on who you talk to, there are multiple numbers of gender identifications. It is more than just being a man or a woman. Some people identify as some kind of animal. Some identify as a fictitious character in a comic book. This gender issue has caused problems between parents and schools, children and parents, along with a host of other problems.

Because of all this confusion and ungodly misinformation, it is important that those who are believers in Jesus declare with confidence and clarity who we are. For us, there is no question about who we are. Look how the Word of God identifies us.

We are witnesses to Christ. Acts 1:8 states:

"But you will receive power when the Holy Spirit has come upon you, and you will be my witnesses in Jerusalem and in all Judea and Samaria, and to the end of the earth."

-(ESV)

Notice that this verse is not a command. It simply reveals the natural outcome of our lives when the Holy Spirit comes to us. The result of His presence in our lives is that we will be witnesses to Christ.

We are the temple of the Holy Spirit. 1 Corinthians 6;19-20 says,

"Or do you not know that your body is a temple of the Holy Spirit within you, whom you have from

God? You are not your own, for you were bought with a price."

The Holy Spirit moved into our lives the moment we believed in Jesus. He is in us to empower us to glorify Christ in all we do.

We are witnesses to his great love for us. It is really impossible to live out the Christian life without telling of the love of God. Our lives have been so overpowered by this love that we can't help but tell others about it. It was a love that compelled Him to leave heaven and come down to get us out of sin. It was a love that compelled him to do something about the condition we were in. It was a love that compelled Him to go to the cross and take upon himself all of my sins and the sins of the world. We give witness to that love.

We are witnesses to the fact that if there are going to be any changes in our society, it is only going to come through Jesus. The healing for racial tension is found only in Jesus. It is when red, yellow, black, and white come to the cross that they find that everyone is on equal and level ground. Skin color and ethnicity are irrelevant at the cross. We are all sinners in need of a savior. We all receive the same forgiveness. We all are covered by the same blood. We all receive the same salvation. It is at the cross we are made brothers and sisters in Christ. We are not going to solve the racial issues through politics, police reform, improved education, or even economic justice. We are going to find the solution only through the cross of Jesus.

Not only are we witnesses of the love of Christ, but we are also the salt of the earth. Jesus said:

"You are the salt of the earth, but if the salt has lost its taste, how shall its saltiness be restored. It is no longer

good for anything except to be thrown out and trampled under people's feet."

-(Matt 5:13) (ESV)

We all know that if you want to change the taste or the flavor of something, just add salt to it. It is an agent of change. It is distinctive in its taste and uses. It keeps food from becoming corrupt or rotten. Salt penetrates food to preserve it. Salt adds flavor.

Jesus said this is what I have made you. I made you to go out into the community and keep it from becoming rotten. I sent you to add flavor to the environment around you by your life and your testimony. I sent you to penetrate into the community. Students penetrate the schools they are in. Employees penetrate their jobs and workplaces. We penetrate those areas by our presence, our witness, and our love for those around us. So, if we want to change the environments we are in, then we must be salt.

Jesus said that He made us the light of the world. A light shines in the darkness. A light gives direction and reveals the dangers ahead. The source of our light is the person of Jesus, who lives in us. So, let us pray that the Holy Spirit will move in our hearts to let the light of Jesus shine through to those around us.

We are the peacemakers. In this time of violence, tension, and destruction, we are to be the peacemakers. The way that we bring peace is by pointing men and women to the one who is the prince of peace. We introduce them to Jesus, who is able to bring calm into their lives right in the center of the social, racial, and political storms.

Christians are called to be peacemakers on college campuses that are in chaos.

Christians are called to be peacemakers in the midst of political unrest by showing love, respect, and kindness to those who have a different opinion than we do.

Christians are to be peacemakers to families in chaos.

Christian young people are called to be peacemakers in schools that have student unrest.

You might ask, "How can we be peacemakers in a troubled world?" We can be peacemakers when we allow the great peacemaker who lives inside of us to bring calm to troubled moments.

These characteristics reveal why we are here. I know that times can be hard and tough, but remember that tough times are one of the reasons why we are here. So may we live out the truth of who we are during these savage times.

Chapter 2: Weeping For America

"And when he drew near and saw the city, he wept over it, saying, "Would that you, even you, had known on this day the things that make for peace!

But now they are hidden from your eyes. For the days will come upon you when your enemies will set up a barricade around you and surround you and hem you in on every side and tear you down to the ground, you and your children within you.

And they will not leave one stone upon another in you because you did not know the time of your visitation."
LUKE 10:41-48

Jesus Coming Into Jerusalem

This passage begins the record of what Jesus experienced in the last week of His life. The whole account of that last week is passionate, powerful, sad, and yet wonderful. It is sad to see that there are two groups of people who are greeting Jesus as He enters Jerusalem.

First, there is the crowd that is cheering Him, waving palm branches to celebrate His arrival. Led by the disciples, the multitude joined in the shouting, blessed is the king who comes in the name of the Lord. Peace in heaven and glory in the highest. The people who were shouting and praising the coming of Jesus into Jerusalem were those who witnessed some of the miracles that Jesus did. Some of them may have been among the 5000 or the 4000 who were fed. Others may have been on the hillside where they heard Jesus speak and teach the Beatitudes. Others may have witnessed Jesus' healing someone or raising someone from the dead. And it could be that in the crowd were those who the Lord had healed. There may have been others who were delivered from demon possession. So, if these people were in that crowd, they had reason to shout and celebrate.

We Have Reason To Celebrate Every Time We Get Together

Think about all of the things that we can testify to in our lives. Think about the time the Lord saved you from your sins. Think about the fact that God Himself lives in your body through the presence of the Holy Spirit. Think about the fact that he sees us and is aware of all we go through.

I love the passage of scripture in Exodus where the Lord is speaking to Moses. He says something that is so important. He says to Moses,

"I have seen the affliction of my people, and I am come down to deliver them."

-(Exodus 3:7) ESV

Isn't that a great verse? I have seen the affliction of my people. If you are hurting, He sees you. If you feel abandoned by family and friends, He sees you. If you have doubts and confusion, He sees you. If your home is not what it should be, He sees you. If you have fallen into sinful behavior, He sees you, not to judge you, but to forgive you and lift you up.

I love movies because I always find scenes or conversations that teach a Biblical principle. One of my favorite movies is Avatar. It is a science fiction movie about a race of people on a distant planet called the NAVI. In their relation to one another, they use an expression that says, I

SEE YOU. This is more than just recognizing your presence. It means that I see more than just the outside. It means that I see your pain. I see your joy. I know what you are going through. I celebrate your joy. But it is a word that means more than just watching from a distance; I am involved with you.

This is what God meant when He said to Moses,

"I have seen the affliction of my people."

He said I know what they are going through. I know the pain they are experiencing now. I know the hardship the Pharaoh is putting them through. I know they feel forgotten and hopeless. So, I'm coming down to deliver them.

Knowing that God sees us that way gives us a reason to celebrate. He knows the intimate details of our lives, and He knows how to help, encourage, and give us what we need.

There Were Enemies Of Jesus In That Crowd

At the same time, there is another group of men welcoming Him, but their welcome is not one of praise; it is one of anger. They complain to Jesus about what the people are saying. They tell Jesus to rebuke His disciples. They did not want them to claim that Jesus came from God. They did not want the people to believe that Jesus was the Messiah. Jesus knew that these religious leaders put a bounty on Him and were looking for a way to kill Him. Even knowing this, Jesus was not going to be intimidated by these hypocritical leaders.

Jesus reminded these hateful men that it was impossible to keep people from praising Him. He said that if they don't praise me, the rocks and the stones will praise me. I would love to have seen the faces of those religious leaders when He said that. We know that through the week, their anger grew as each day moved toward the cross.

"When Jesus got to the top of the hill, He wept."

-(41-44)

One would think that the large crowd that greeted Jesus would have pleased Him. It would have made his heart glad, but it did not. The reason it did not give Him joy was because He knew that in just a few days, another crowd would gather and call for His execution. Could it be that some of the people in the crowd celebrating His arrival would be in the crowd later in the week demanding his death? Maybe.

Jesus Wept Because The City And The People Rejected Him

Jesus knew that the celebration of the crowds was just transitory. It would not last. Jesus knew that the city and the people rejected Him. He knew that they were going to nail Him to a cross. Looking at the city and knowing the rejection, He wept. This weeping was not just silent tears, but the words used here mean that Jesus burst into tears. He was crying out loud and someone who was deeply grieving. He was heartbroken over the spiritual condition of the city.

Jerusalem experienced the favor and love of God. The history of the city shows how God blessed her. It was the city of David, the king who was called "a man after God's own heart." It was a city blessed with the great prophets of God, Isaiah and Jeremiah. It was blessed by the presence of the temple of God, which symbolized the presence of God. Finally, it was a city honored by the coming of Christ. Sadly, the city turned its back on these privileges and rejected the

Son of God. Jesus knew all of this as He looked over the city. In that moment, He reacted with gut-wrenching grief.

Jesus Wept Because Of How Sinful The City Became

Even though Jerusalem was the favored city of God, it proved to be a city where the people were most ungrateful and rebellious. As one writer says,

"The Most favored people in the world crowned their guilt by crucifying the Son of God."

-(W.F. Adeney, The Pulpit Commentary Gospel of Matthew, Copyright © 2001, 2003, 2005, 2006, 2010 by Biblesoft, Inc.)

Jesus Wept Because The City Was Doomed

In His mind, he looked into the future and saw this beautiful city destroyed. The temple, which shone brilliantly in the sunlight, would be destroyed. Jesus told His disciples that the day was coming when the temple would be torn down stone by stone. This prophecy was fulfilled in 70 A.D. when Titus besieged the city and eventually destroyed it. When the Roman soldiers set fire to the temple, all of the gold that was inside of it began to melt. The melted gold began to run between the stones. The soldiers, seeing this, began to tear the stones down to get to the gold. Even though Titus commanded that the temple not be touched, it was completely destroyed and the Roman soldiers looted the gold and other valuable treasure.
(BiblicalHermeneuticsstackexchange.com, 2024)

Jesus knew that continued rebellion against God always resulted in destruction of some kind. This was the lesson taught in the Old Testament. The Apostle Paul stated that the stories found in the Old Testament are there for us to learn from. The Jews had a history of rebelling against the Lord and then experiencing His discipline. Sometimes, the discipline was harsh in that it led to captivity. The point of all these stories is to remind us that there are serious consequences when we decide we are not going to follow the teachings of scripture.

Sadly, our nation and society are making decisions that are in complete rejection and disobedience to the word of God. Here are some of those national decisions that are contrary to the Word of God.

The Redefining Of Marriage

For generations, marriage was described as a union between a man and a woman. That definition has changed. Marriage is now defined as the union between two or more people regardless of sex or gender. Marriage now includes homosexual and gay relationships as marriage. Modern society now accepts marriage in whatever way someone wants to define it.

The Devaluing Of The Unborn

There is such a push for abortion that it is now considered to be one of the most important topics or issues in modern-day elections. One writer said that the push for abortion is the celebration and the encouragement of death for the unborn child. Of course, those who push for abortion do not believe that the unborn child is a person yet. So, since the unborn child is not a person, then destroying it is nothing to be concerned about.

This devaluing of the unborn life was seen at the recent Democratic National Convention, where Planned Parenthood had a mobile medical unit that was offering free abortions for anyone who wanted one. Lila Rose, an opinion writer, said, "As the DNC unfolds in Chicago this week, the true agenda of the abortion industry is on full display -- an agenda that seeks to convince people that pregnancy is a disease and that motherhood is a curse. These are lies, plain and simple. Motherhood and family are some of the most meaningful and beautiful experiences anyone can have, bringing joy and fulfillment. But the DNC, backed by the abortion industry, has chosen a different path, one that celebrates the killing of innocent children as some twisted form of empowerment. The act of ending a human life has been trivialized to the point of absurdity, packaged as some sort of liberation for women. But there is no freedom in killing your child—only slavery to an anti-life ideology that tells women that motherhood is something to be feared and avoided at all costs." *(The DNC Hellish Abortion Rituals; The celebration of Death, The real agenda, Lila Rose, Fox News Digital,* MSN.com)

The Refusal To Enforce Laws That Protect Citizens

This refusal violates God's design for government. Romans 13 gives God instructions for the government. The government was designed to protect citizens by enforcing laws. When laws are not enforced, anarchy ensues, and innocent civilians become at risk.

Sadly, we are now in a time when those who are policemen and police women are denigrated for the job they do. Assaults and attacks on police are now common. Videos are taken of police officers being attacked and beaten by gangs of men. Some of these men are taken into custody and then released without bail.

Perpetrators who have raped or molested women have been released back into public life, where many times, they commit the same crimes on a different victim. We have politicians who have contributed to the bail release of those who were involved in riots and also assaulted police. One young woman was videoed spitting in the face of an officer. She was immediately handcuffed and taken to jail. As she was handcuffed, she could be heard screaming that this should not be happening. She was taken, booked, and then released. When she was released, her friends greeted her as some kind of hero.

These are just a few illustrations of how our society is rebelling against the laws of God. Jesus knew that the rebellion and rejection of Jerusalem were going to result in her destruction. How, then, do we expect to escape the judgment of God when we are doing the same thing as Jerusalem did in this passage?

There Is Time To Repent

When Jesus looked over Jerusalem and wept, He gave an invitation. He exposed His heart and His love for the people. In Matthew 23:37, Jesus said,

"O Jerusalem, Jerusalem, the city that kills the prophets and stones those who are sent to it! How often would I

have gathered your children together as a hen gathers her brood under her wings, and you were not willing!"

-(ESV)

"Notice the heart of Jesus when He says, '**I would have gathered your children as a hen gathers her brood.**''This is a phrase that means belonging, closeness, and protection. This could have been the experience of the city, but they were not willing.

Could it be that we are seeing this within our own nation? The gospel is being presented on multiple radio and television stations. There is a church on almost every corner in every city. Yet, the gospel is being rejected and neglected. Many people no longer consider themselves to be a part of any church or denomination. A growing number of people consider themselves to be "nones," meaning that they do not have any particular religious beliefs.

There Will Come A Time When The Opportunity To Be Saved Will Be Gone

Jesus said that the reason the people of Jerusalem were going to be destroyed was because "**they did not recognize the time of their visitation.**" They did not recognize or accept who He was. They refused His message, His life, His miracles, and who he claimed to be. Their rejection was filled with hate, so much hate that they were willing to release a notorious killer for a loving, caring Messiah.

Like Jerusalem, we, too, as a nation, may be facing a time when it will be too late. When the present policies cause our nation to continue to deteriorate morally, spiritually, and socially, we should not be surprised that God will tire of it and bring down His judgment on America. We may not know what that judgment will entail, but we will know the reason. We rejected and rebelled against God. This should cause all believers to grieve over the condition of our country and pray that God will bring a spiritual awakening.

Those Of Us Who Are Believers Need To Weep Over Those Who Are Rejecting Jesus

More and more people are rejecting Jesus as the Messiah. They are rejecting that there was anything significant about His cross. He was just a good man who was executed. He was a good teacher whose teachings were rejected. And then others claim that Jesus was mentally ill for claiming He was the son of God.

There needs to be sadness in us because of loved ones who do not know Christ. We need to grieve over the fact that there are so many people who are looking for other ways to find God than the right way.

Jesus wept while the city was feasting and being in a party mood.

One writer said that the whole atmosphere was like a present-day convention. People were celebrating the coming Passover. They were meeting with family and friends to prepare, and there was a sense of excitement about the Passover event. While this was going on, Jesus was weeping over the city and the people.

It is important that those of us in the church understand the spiritual condition of our community and our culture. We also have those who reject anything that has to do with the church and spiritual matters. They see the bright and shining things that Satan flashes in front of them, and they chase after it. Soon, those bright and shiny objects become corrupted and damaging to the lives of those who follow them. Soon, the party will be over, and the individual ends up with a broken life. It should cause us sadness to know that there are so many of our friends and loved ones who are choosing a path that leads them to destruction, not life. The primary reason people are rejecting the message of Jesus is because they chose not to hear it.

Jesus Wept Because Of The Hardness Of People's Hearts

One of the most amazing things about this last week in Jesus' life is how fickle the people were. Here they were celebrating, but on Friday, they will be screaming in rage for Jesus to be crucified. On Sunday, they are shouting Hosanna, blessed is He who comes in the name of the Lord. On Friday, they will demand He be crucified.

Today, we too, are witnessing the hardness of people's hearts in the midst of our political area. I learned through the years that there is very little unifying in politics. The whole purpose of politics is division. People who are on opposite sides of a political discussion treat each other more like enemies than friends.

We witnessed recently what happens when there are hateful words spoken. When hyperbolic statements are made, someone is going to take it upon themselves to fix the problem. Former President Trump has been called a threat to democracy; He has the Heart of Hitler. He is going to end elections and so many other hateful things. A young man hears that and thinks he is going to save the country from this madman and attempts to kill him.

Former President Trump is not innocent of incendiary language. He calls people mocking and humiliating names when they disagree with him. Those who were supporters have received his wrath if they did something he did not approve of. The point is that there are awful conversations happening in our political world that have been happening for a long time. And there are consequences to that rhetoric. Sometimes, those consequences are deadly.

Hard Hearts Are Not Limited To Politics

Hard hearts can also be found in the church. I was called to a church that had vicious, marathon business meetings that lasted late into the night. Men and women who were brothers and sisters in Christ would say things to one another that should never be said. I heard church members call each other names and spread false statements about other members. I think this is the kind of thing that makes Jesus weep. It is to see the hard-heartedness of his people. This should break our hearts as well.

Jesus Wept Because The People Had No Spiritual Leaders

Jesus blasted the religious leaders for not giving the people what they needed. They, instead burdened down the people with ridiculous rules and regulations. They threatened to excommunicate the people if they disagreed with the leadership. They rejected the miracles that Jesus did. They called Him a disciple of Satan. He was accused of blasphemy.

When Jesus saw the 5000 in the wilderness, the Bible says that Jesus had mercy on them because they were like sheep without a shepherd. Because the people did not have the right kind of spiritual leadership, they could not find the peace God promised them.

Our Spiritual Leadership Is Questionable Today

Presently, the church is falling in attendance of members. There are many churches that are closing their doors. There are pastors who believe that there is more than one way to get to heaven. Some even teach that Christianity and Islam are very similar in their theology. Jesus said that the success of any ministry is lifting Him up and pointing to the cross. He said that when the church does that, then many people are going to be drawn to Him. The church needs men like John the Baptist, who was described as a "voice crying in the wilderness." Let us pray that there can be voices crying out from the pulpits, but that those of us who are Christians can be that voice that cries out in the darkness. May we be that light that points me and women to Christ. May we be the salt that gives a good flavor to our community?

Let us pray that this sadness that Jesus had as He looked over Jerusalem becomes our sadness as we look over our nation.

May we be like Jeremiah, who said that he does not have enough tears to cry for his people.

May we be like Paul, who said that he would suffer condemnation if the people of Israel were saved.

May we take the example of the young fireman who threw his body over his wife and daughter to save them from the shooter who tried to assassinate President Trump. He sacrificed his life so his family could be saved. May we sacrifice our time and our money for the cause of Christ. May we spend intentional time reading and studying the Word of God so we can help those who are lost find Christ.

Chapter 3: A Prayer For America

"To the choirmaster. A Psalm of the Sons of Korah. LORD, you were favorable to your land; you restored the fortunes of Jacob."

-Psalm 85:1-6

"You forgave the iniquity of your people; you covered all their sin. *Selah.*"

<u>-Psa 85:2</u>

"You withdrew all your wrath; you turned from your hot anger."

<u>-Psa 85:3</u>

"Restore us again, O God of our salvation, and put away your indignation toward us!"

<u>-Psa 85:4</u>

"Will you be angry with us forever? Will you prolong your anger to all generations?"

<u>-Psa 85:5</u>

"Will you not revive us again, that your people may rejoice in you?"

<u>-Psa 85:6</u>

This Psalm is the prayer of a man who loves his country. He is praying for God to do a wonderful work, and the work he is praying for is revival. He knows that the people of God have been rebellious. He acknowledges that God is angry with them because of their sinful behavior, their idolatry, their rebellion, their rejection of his word, and their corruption of worship. He knows that the problems that they have with government, economics, education and politics are the results of men and women turning away from the Lord. He comes before the Lord on behalf of his country and asks God to restore them, to revive them, and to bring them back into a right relationship with him.

We find that our own nation is at the very same crossroads that Israel was in this passage of scripture. We are experiencing the same kinds of problems and we are experiencing these problems for the very same reason.

We have fallen so far in regard to human life that we now place animals above human beings. Did you know that in the United States of America, if you willfully and deliberately destroy the egg of an eagle, You could be fined $5,000 dollars and put in prison for a year. For destroying the egg of an eagle! Some environmentalists might say, "Well, of course. There's a little baby eagle in there." Yet a doctor can take the life of an unborn child and kill it and be considered a friend of women's rights.

These are just some of the issues that we are facing. These issues are a reflection of the attitude of people toward God. For many today, God is an afterthought. He is someone you think about if there is a 9/11 or if there is some kind of serious illness or a tragedy. When times are hard and tough then we give our attention to God.

This Psalm was written as a Song of Thanksgiving for God's deliverance and restoration of His people. They had a history of sin and rebellion against God. Because of that sin, God disciplined them by sending them into captivity. Now they have returned, and the Psalmist is reflecting on all of the things God has done for the nation.

This Psalm could have been written about God's relationship with our own country. God has blessed us throughout the years of our history. It is easy to look back at the history of our country and recognize the blessings God gave us and continues to give us.

He gave us great leaders at just the right time to gain our independence.

He gave us great spiritual leaders who guided us through revivals and spiritual awakenings.

He gave us unity after a war divided us over slavery and oppression.

He gave us a land full of natural resources.

He gave us His grace continually through the years.

An entire book could be written just listing the blessings of God on America.

The Psalmist Celebrates The Continual Blessings Of God

The Psalmist begins with this statement: "Lord, you have poured out blessing on our land."

I believe that America is the most blessed country in the world. Above, we spoke about the blessings of natural resources God gave us. We have such an abundance of natural resources that we share with the world. Because America has been such a generous country, many of these resources go to help developing nations or those nations that don't have the resources we have.

He blessed us with the ability and the desire to educate every child born in America. It is true that we have problems in our education system. It is also true that our students are falling behind the rest of the world in subjects like math, science, and technology. In spite of those shortcomings, we are great in that we educate everyone. Every child has the opportunity to learn and earn a degree of some kind. No one is turned away from school because of their wealth, social status, or mental ability. Even those children who recently entered our country illegally are able to be admitted to schools.

We have the greatest standard of living in the world. This is why thousands and thousands of people are trying to get into our country. They want a better life. The border is now filled with unaccompanied children. Parents have sent their children to the United States, hoping that they will have a better life than they have. They want what we have. Even the poorest American has much more than many in the rest of the world.

We are blessed with the best medical care in the world. We have researchers who are finding cures for the worst of diseases. I heard this week of a chip that is being developed to help those with spinal injuries be able to walk. Yes, we have problems in some of our health care, but compared to the rest of the world, we have the best.

We are blessed in that we had men who had their priorities right in the founding of this nation. God gave us leaders like George Washington, John Adams, Patrick Henry, James Madison, Benjamin Rush, and so many others to lead in the founding of this nation. He gave us men who were willing to pledge their lives, their fortunes, and their sacred honor for the freedom of this country. He gave us men who knew that the success of America was never going to be dependent on their own ability and resources, but it was going to come from our dependence on God.

Roger Batson was a sociologist who was doing a study on the development of America compared to the development of other countries in the Western Hemisphere. While interviewing a South American President he made a comparison to the resources of America compared to the resources and the development of the countries in Central and South America. He said that South America is like America in many ways. It has natural resources and wonderful people, and yet it has lagged behind America in almost everything. "Why is that?" he asked. The South American President gave a very profound answer. He said that the reason America has achieved all that it has is because of the kind of beginning it had. He said, "Those who settled in South America came to South America because they were seeking gold. Those who came to North America came to North America because they were seeking God."

When the Pilgrims landed on Plymouth Rock in Massachusetts, they wrote the Mayflower Compact. The beginning words of that document said, "For the glory of God and the advancement of the Christian Faith."

When the founding Fathers wrote the Declaration of Independence, they wrote, "We hold these truths to be self-evident that all men are endowed by their creator with certain unalienable rights." Our founding Fathers believed in a creator. They believed that it was God who gave rights to men, not the government. They believed that God provided resources to men, not the government. Because it is God who gives these rights, the government does not have the right to take them away.

These are just some of the blessings God has given to us as a nation. But it seems that we have become prideful and arrogant. We are saying that we don't need God. We have everything under control. There are those in our culture today who want us to move away from Biblical teaching and accept more modern policies like DEI (Diversity, Equity, and Inclusion) and CRT (Critical Race Theory). We shall speak more about these policies later, but both of these policies contradict what the Bible says about individuals and how they are to interact in society. Both of these programs have disrupted the organization and the effectiveness of major institutions, education, police departments, and adult and youth sports. Both of these policy programs deny the Biblical definition of gender. They are programs that create victims and perpetrators based on the color of their skin. The Bible, on the other hand, teaches that a person is never valued based on the color of their skin or their ethnicity. The value of every human being is based on the value God gives us.

There have been concerted efforts by some leaders to remove the mention of God from schools, city council meetings, and other government agencies. I used to say that we have removed God from the classroom, the courtroom, and politics. In reality, removing God from anywhere is not even possible. God does not stop at the entrance to a school because we have kicked Him out. The reality is that God never left. We might ignore Him and not have anything to do with Him while we are at school and at the office, but ignoring Him does not mean He is not there. He is present with us even when we don't want Him.

Some school administrators passed a policy that says there cannot be prayer in school. In reality, it is impossible to keep a student from praying in school. One comedian said that as long as there are tests in school, there will always be prayer. The good news is that God has not left any of these places where we tried to remove Him. He is still in the classroom. He is still in the courtroom and the Congress of the United States. He is still here, and thankfully, He is not going anywhere. Our society and culture may have rejected Him, but that rejection does not drive Him away. He is still here because He loves us and wants us to know Him.

It has become unacceptable to mention His name in some public meetings. Crosses that have been present for years are now seen to be offensive to those who are not Christian. The Ten Commandments have been removed from courthouses because they may influence jurors who are deliberating cases. Signs, symbols, and artwork are either removed or covered up because some may be offensive to those who are not Christians. Christian athletes have been mocked and criticized for demonstrating their faith in public. Christian athletes, Christian politicians, and other Christian community leaders are asked to be silent about their faith while at the same time celebrating those athletes who announce they are gay. We celebrate those who have changed their gender identity, but a Christian athlete is criticized because they identify with Christ. A biological man identifying as a woman is okay. A student who identifies as a cat, a rabbit, or some other kind of animal is encouraged. But Christians are scorned and mocked because of their identity in Christ.

It is as though we have reached a point in time when we don't want to acknowledge the truth that we are great because God has made us great. We are blessed because God has blessed us. The writer of this passage says you POURED out your blessings. God has literally poured out on us His grace and blessings. We need to acknowledge him for what He has done.

The Psalmist Prays For The Nation To Be Restored (4)

The restoration the Psalmist is asking for is the restoration from captivity. He is asking that the people of Israel be allowed to return home. Like the captives mentioned in this passage, we also have men and women who are captive. Several American citizens are being held captive or in prison in other countries. Some of them have been falsely accused of some contrived crime. Their family and friends are praying that they be restored to their families. These men and women pray to return home and be restored to their freedom and their family.

However, there is another kind of restoration I want us to consider. That is the need for a Spiritual Restoration. We need to be restored in our spiritual practices and disciplines. We need to be restored in the practice and participation in worship. Sadly, fewer and fewer people consider church and worship to be something of a priority in their lives. Average church attendance across denominational lines is decreasing every year. More and more people are becoming inactive and inattentive to worship. Thousands of churches close every year, and there is a shortage of spiritual leadership. There are fewer men accepting the call of God to become pastors and church leaders. The general attitude toward the church is that of indifference. Many people just do not feel the need for the church and think that the church no longer has relevance in our modern society.

This indifference is not just found among those who are not Christians, but it is all found among many who claim to be Christians. The majority of men and women who say they are Christian do not participate in worship and fellowship of a local church. This decline escalated since COVID. According to Lifeway Research 4500 churches closed in 2023. Church attendance has been lower since the Pandemic. Research showed that men and women got out of the habit of going to church and failed to return. (The Houston Herald; "Thousands of churches are closing every year," by the Herald Staff, January 26, 2023)

The only thing that is going to change this attitude among Christians is a spiritual awakening or revival among the people of God. We need a spiritual renewal in this country. We need a revival of the people of God. We cannot expect our nation to experience any kind of change in our society and culture without a spiritual awakening or revival. So may we join the Psalmist in asking God to restore the spiritual vitality of our nation.

Pray that we will remember where we came from. Sadly, we have our history being revised. Our young people do not know who our founders were. They don't know the heroes of this country. They can tell you the theme song to Frozen or some other movie, but they do not know anything about Thomas Paine, Benjamin Franklin, or Thomas Jefferson. They are not familiar with the sacrifices that we made to bring about our independence as a nation. If we are not taught about our history, then we will raise a generation of students who will not have an appreciation for our country. When they are not exposed to the kinds of sacrifices that our Founding Fathers made, then they can be easily misled by those who hold to Marxism and socialism as an alternative political form. When students are not taught about the exceptionalism of America, then they will not learn to love their country.

The results of history not being taught were seen on our college campuses these past two years as students burned the flag, took over college common areas, and spewed their hate of America. Some college professors believe that America needs to be "burned to the ground" so another more acceptable nation can be formed.

When Thomas Jefferson was a student, he copied the following quote and kept it in his journal: *"A government is like everything else: to preserve it, we must love it."* This was a quote from the great political philosopher Montesquieu. The passage continued by saying, "Everything, therefore, depends on establishing this love in a republic." "And to inspire it ought to be the principal business of education." If Jefferson were alive today, he might say to our education system, "You had one job to do, and you failed." (The New York Post; "Public Schools are teaching our children to hate America," Mary Kay Linge, February 22, 2020). Instead of producing patriots and lovers of the Republic, we are creating angry young people who have a desire to tear down the government that gave them the education they received.

One commentator said that the biggest problem that faces America today is ignorance and apathy. This can lead to the loss of freedom and liberty. One of our founding pastors said that it is easier to take liberty from an ignorant person than it is to steal the wallet of a blind man. We need to continually educate our children in the truths about the founding of our country.

Not only do we need to know the facts about the founding of our country, but we need to be aware of how current events are shaping America. We need to know how different laws affect the family, religious freedom, and worship. We need to understand how certain laws are violating the rights of conscience. Let us pray that we will be people who are knowledgeable of current events and care about the things that are developing in our country.

The Founding Principles Of Our Nation

I want to remind you, dear reader, that our nation was born in the heat of a spiritual revival. Of the 55 men who were framers of the Constitution, fifty of them were professing Christians. Thirty of them were bold Christians. James Madison, the architect of the federal constitution and the fourth president of the United States, said, "We've staked the whole future of American civilization, not upon the power of government. Far from it. We have staked the future upon the capacity of each and every one of us to govern ourselves, to sustain ourselves according to the 10 Commandments of God."

George Washington is the one who knelt in the snow at Valley Forge and prayed God's blessing on his rag-tag continental army, and God gave a victory. When a visitor visited the Continental Congress, he was sitting in the gallery. He wanted to know which one was George Washington. The man next to him said, "George Washington will be the tall man that gets on his knees when Congress goes to pray. That's the kind of birth that we've had.

In December of 1820, Daniel Webster said, "Let us not forget the religious character of our origin." We are facing the danger of forgetting the religious character of our beginning. Revisionist historians are so committed to political correctness that they don't want to mention the kind of impact the Bible and Christian faith had on the founding of our nation. Our Founding Fathers quoted the Bible. They based their writings on the word of God. We need to be reminded of how much our Founding Fathers depended on God to help us win our independence.

John Quincy Adams, in 1821, said this about the American Revolution, "The highest glory of the American Revolution was this it connected with the principles of Christianity." Did you hear that? The Founding Fathers believed that there was a connection between the principles of Christianity and the principles of government. Our forefathers believed in the separation of church and state, but they never believed in the separation of God from government. Never.

As a matter of fact, John Adams believed that the two most important holidays in the young nation were the celebration of Christmas and the celebration of the 4th of July. He said that we celebrate Christmas because of the birth of the Son of God. He went on to say that we celebrate the 4th of July because a nation was born that depended on God.

No nation ever had the kind of a beginning that our nation had. John Quincy Adams went on to say, "From the day of the declaration, we were bound by the laws of God and by the laws of the gospel which rules our conduct."

On June 8, 1845, President Andrew Jackson said, "The Bible is the rock upon which our republic stands." That's not some Baptist preacher saying that. That's Andrew Jackson. "The Bible is the rock upon which our republic stands."

Abraham Lincoln, in 1861, as he was bidding his farewell in Springfield, Illinois, said this, "Unless the great God that assisted Washington shall be with me, and aid me, I must fail. But if the same omniscient mind and mighty arm that directed and protected him shall guide and support me, I shall not fail. In regards to this Bible, Lincoln said it is the best gift God has given to men. All the good the Savior gave to the world was communicated in this book. If not for it, we would not know right from wrong. "

In 1941, President Woodrow Wilson said, "America was born to exemplify devotion to the elements of righteousness which are derived in the Holy Scriptures." This is our birthright to practice the righteousness which was born in the Holy Scriptures.

In 1952, Supreme Court Justice William O Douglas said, "We are religious people, and our institutions presuppose a supreme being. You tell that to the ACLU. You tell that to other people who will make us believe that somehow, we've not come from this kind of background. "

In 1954 President Dwight D. Eisenhower said, "The purpose of a devout and united people was set forth in the pages of the Bible, to live in freedom, to work in a prosperous land and to obey the commandments of God."

In June 1954, Congress adopted the phrase "Under God" to be put into the Pledge of Allegiance.

And in 1956, not so very long ago, by a joint resolution, Congress had adopted the bill making the national motto of the United States of America this, "In God We Trust."

Ronald Reagan rightly said, "The time has come to turn to God and reassert our trust in Him for the healing of

America. Our country is in need and ready for a spiritual renewal."

This is our history. We need a restoration and an adequate understanding of our history. If we don't learn and remember how we were founded, we will continue down the path of our own destruction. It is a path that says we don't need God. We can do it on our own. If we continue down that road, then we will face severe judgment and the possible destruction of our way of life.

I Love This Country

I love to hear these patriotic songs that we sang today. I love to see the flag fly. I get a lump in my throat when I see wounded warriors or when I see videos of soldiers coming home and surprising their children. I love to read about our history and see all that we have come through. I believe that it is Biblical to be patriotic and love your country.

Now, saying I love my country doesn't mean I don't love other countries. When I want God to bless America, that doesn't mean that I don't want other countries to be blessed, it just means that America is my fatherland. This is the land of my birth and this is the land of my loyalty and the land of my responsibility.

We Must Pray To Be Revived

In verse 6, the Psalmist prays for revival. This means that he is praying for the people of God to be stirred in their personal commitment to God. He prays that the people of God will be revived in their love for God, their love for worship. He prays that they will be revived in their passion for righteousness. I think about this and feel that this should

40

be the prayer of God's people. Lord, revive us. Revive our love and passion for you. Revive our priorities toward you.

The Psalmist says, "Revive us that so your people can rejoice in you." The children of Israel were rejoicing in their material prosperity. They were rejoicing in the goodness of their economy, the strength of their military, and the security of the temple. They were rejoicing in their own ingenuity and power. This is the same thing that is happening in our own country today. We rejoice in all of the resources we have. We rejoice in the freedom and liberty we have. We rejoice in our material blessings, our bank accounts, our retirement our possessions.

The writer of this Psalm says, "Lord, we need to change what makes us full of joy." He says revive us so we can rejoice in you. He prays for a revival of our love for Christ, our love for fellowship with Him. If this revival does not take place, then I fear what will happen to our country. If the people of God are not revived in their love for Christ, I fear the future. So, let us pray for a revival among the people of God.

When this revival takes place, then we will see a wonderful change in this country that we love so much.

Chapter 4: America The Beautiful

This is an American patriotic song written by a young teacher by the name of Katharine Lee Bates. The music was composed by a church organist, Samuel A Ward, at Grace Episcopal Church in Newark, New Jersey. These two people were responsible for one of the greatest American songs ever written.

Bates was a professor of English Literature at Wellesley College who was invited to Colorado to give a lecture. As her time was about to end, she and some friends decided to take a trip to the top of Pikes Peak. She and her friends rode wagons and eventually mules to reach the top. While there, the sky was clear, and it was as if she could see from sea to shining sea. The view gave inspiration to the song which eventually became known as America the Beautiful.

She describes her experience and what she saw from the top of Pikes Peak. *"One day, some of the other teachers and I decided to go on a trip to 14,000-foot Pikes Peak. We hired a prairie wagon. Near the top, we had to leave the wagon and go the rest of the way on mules. I was very tired. But when I saw the view, I felt great joy. All the wonder of America seemed displayed there, with the sea-like expanse."* *(The balladofAmerica.org; America the Beautiful; About the Song.)*

I want to spend some time working through the lyrics and see not just the beauty of the song but the idea of America that came from the mind of God.

The British writer G. K. Chesterton visited the United States for the first time and remarked that America was "a nation with the soul of a church," not because of its religiosity but because of a common creed enshrined in "sacred texts" of the Declaration of Independence and Constitution. Ms. Bates seemed to capture that same idea with the lyrics of her song.

The first verse describes God's graceful artwork in America

O beautiful for spacious skies, for amber waves of grain

For purple mountain majesties, above the fruited plain

America, America, God shed His grace on thee

And crown thy good with brotherhood, from sea to shining sea

The first verse describes the beauty of the American landscape. As Miss Bates traveled to Colorado, she traveled through the wheat fields of Kansas and looked at the golden stalks that went on for miles and miles. When the train she was on began to ascend the lower Rocky Mountains, she felt as if she was moving ever closer to the presence of God. The majestic snow-covered mountains and the majesty of the scenery took her breath away.

As she wrote that first verse, it was as if she was celebrating God's handiwork. She was adding to what the Psalmist said when he wrote the heavens declare the glory of God and the earth shows His handiwork.

She must have wondered how anyone could live in such a marvelous and majestic place and not see the work of God. How could anyone look from Pikes Peak and not realize that God created this wonderful masterpiece that she was able to see?

The word that came to her mind as she looked at this marvelous land, we call America was grace. It was grace that brought about this beautiful land. It was grace that created this marvelous country. It was grace that provided great leaders and founders. It was grace that reunited a divided nation and ended the horrific practice of slavery. All of this was because of the grace of God.

She writes God shed His grace on thee. The beauty of what she was seeing made her think that God did not just sprinkle His grace on America. He shed His grace; He poured out His grace. And He continues to pour out of His grave.

The song has the elements of a prayer. A prayer of praise for all God has done for America. Her prayer begins with the request that God will crown all with goodness and brotherhood. It is a prayer asking that God will cause men who live in this great land to see His grace, and may they relate to one another with that grace. The grace that makes them brothers.

Over the past several years, some politicians have been talking about reparations that need to be made to the black men and women of our country for the institution of slavery that was a part of our history. Some are saying that some kind of payment must be made to the black community to make up for past atrocities.

I don't believe that making a monetary payment is the way to make reparations for the crime of slavery. The word reparations comes from the word repair. So, it seems to me that the best way to make reparations is to repair the broken relationship between the races. It is when white men and women and black men and women look at each other as brothers and sisters. It's when we stop meeting in segregated houses of worship on Sunday and meet together as a family to worship the Lord.

It is this kind of brotherhood that this song refers to or implies. May we also pray that the grace of God will make us better in our relationships with one another, no matter what race or ethnic group we belong to.

The second verse celebrates those men and women who conquered this land and made it into the nation it is.

O beautiful for Pilgrim feet, whose stern, impassioned stress,

A thoroughfare for freedom beat across the wilderness,

America, America, God mend thine every flaw,

Confirm thy soul in self-control, Thy liberty in law.

We can think of the Pilgrims in this verse. We remember the pilgrims who landed on Plymouth Rock and created a colony of new believers in this new world. We think about the Pilgrims who met in Philadelphia and wrote the Declaration of Independence and, later, the Constitution. We remember the Pilgrims who fought in that war of Independence, who suffered and died at Valley Forge, who endured all kinds of hardship just so they and we could be free. We can be reminded of the Pilgrims who crossed first the Appalachian Mountains, then the Mississippi River and finally reach the Pacific Ocean. We could list many more.

Even though Miss Bates celebrates those founding Pilgrims, she also realizes that they were not perfect men and women. She realized that the men who wrote that all men were created equal did not always practice that belief. Some of them were slave owners. Women at one time did not have the same rights as men, such as the right to vote. Black men and women were only considered 3/4 human. Yes, those who began the country and blazed a path were not perfect. This is why she wrote mend every flaw. It is a prayer that

God help us recognize where we are wrong and make us right.

Today, we can say mend the flaws of abortion.

Mend the flaws of sex trafficking.

Mend the flaws of racism.

Mend the flaws of spiritual indifference.

Mend the flaws of a broken education system that teaches revisionist history.

Mend the flaws of those who do not give honor and allegiance to the greatest country in the world.

She then asks the Lord to give us self-control. Remember, this poem was written after the Civil War. The nation was still trying to recover. So, it was appropriate for her to pray for self-control. It was a prayer asking that we not seek vengeance against each other. It is a reminder that we are understanding and compassionate with one another.

But may we also exercise control in liberty and law. May our laws be just. May they reflect the righteousness of you.

The third verse celebrates the Heroes of America.

O beautiful for heroes proved, in liberating strife

Who more than self their country loved, and mercy more than life

America, America, May God they gold refine

Till all success be nobleness, and every gain divine

I don't know all the heroes she was thinking about, but the words indicate that she was thinking about those who served in the military. These were the men and women who proved who they were because of the battle they fought. She may have been thinking of all the thousands of young men who fought during the War for Independence. These unnamed heroes were the ones who paid the ultimate cost so we could experience freedom and liberty.

We have heroes who were in WWII, Korea, Desert Storm, and Iraqi Freedom. Some were in Afghanistan on multiple tours. Some of you reading this are the heroes she is referring to. You who loved your country more than your own life are the heroes she is referring to. We thank you for the personal sacrifices you made. We grieve with you over any physical, emotional, or mental injuries you experienced. There is no way anyone who has not done what you did or been through what you experienced can know the depth of what you went through. But please know how much we appreciate you for all you have done.

Also, know it is more than just a statement that says thank you for your service; it is a deep gratitude that says we have what we have today because you and others before you made the ultimate sacrifice to make sure that we are able to enjoy the life we have today.

But there are other heroes we could mention: the Heroes who fought for civil rights and the heroes who fought for racial equality. These were the heroes who were put in jail, mocked, beaten, and attacked, but they continued the fight for equality for all men and women in this nation. And they won. It is true that we have witnessed improvements, but we still have a way to go in regard to racial and social justice. But at least there are no longer water fountains and restrooms separated by race. Those of color are no longer required to sit in the back of the bus. Black, Hispanic, and Asian men and women now have the ability to serve in places of leadership and be part of making America a "More Perfect Union."

The last verse is a prayer about our future

O beautiful for patriot dream, that sees beyond the years,

Thine alabaster cities gleam, undimmed by human tears,

America, America, God shed His grace on thee,

And crown thy good with brotherhood, from sea to shining sea.

It is a prayer for those who are thinking ahead. The kind of thinking she is talking about is more than just prosperity, materialism, and ease of living. She is thinking ahead to the continued experience of the grace of God. She is thinking ahead when there will be real brotherhood.

She is thinking ahead to a time when politicians will be able to disagree without the name-calling, the false accusations, the questioning of patriotism, and other behaviors. She is looking ahead to a time when the Spirit of God will rule in the hearts of men to create an even greater America.

May we also be thinking ahead to the time when we will experience a move of God like we have never experienced before. May we look forward to a revival in the church where God's people consider their spiritual life as more important than anything the world has to offer.

Chapter 5: The Greatest Threat To America

As I write this, we are involved in another election cycle for our country. It seems that these election cycles are perpetual in the sense that someone is always running for office of some kind. At the same time, as soon as an election ends, some politicians who lost begin their campaign to regain their seats. We, the public, are constantly dealing with campaign ads, political attacks, and various propaganda from either political activists or a candidate running for office.

During each election cycle, each political party denigrates the other. These political attacks have become more vicious in that now, instead of just disagreeing on certain principles, politicians treat each other as enemies. The personal attacks we are witnessing today are the most extreme I have witnessed in my life. The attacks have become so extreme that political opponents are considered a threat to American Democracy. Families have not been immune to the political divisions. Some have even suggested that family members should lie to one another about who they vote for. Others have stated that if they vote for a particular candidate they are voting against their wives and mothers. Recent political rhetoric has affected family holidays and traditions to where family members refuse to spend holidays together because of the differences of opinion.

What is the greatest threat to America? Well, it depends on who you talk to. If you ask that question to a Democratic strategist, you will probably hear that Donald Trump is the greatest threat to America. If you were to ask a Republican, many will more than likely say that the greatest threat to America is the Liberal Democratic Party. Even though these kinds of attacks are extreme, they are not new. Even the founding fathers had strong words about one another. Our founding fathers understood that even though their opponent had a different view, that did not mean he was being unpatriotic. They knew that every man in government loved America and had proven their love by pledging their life and their fortune for freedom. At the same time, these men, even though differing in opinion on political matters, had faith in this newly established government.

Jonathan Turley, a law professor at George Washington Law School, says, "Today, there appears to be a crisis of faith in government. Many now question democracy as a **sustainable system of government**. It represents the single greatest threat to this nation: a citizenry that has lost faith not just with our system of government but with each other. (Jonathan Turley, "The Greatest Single threat to America is hiding in plain sight," Fox News Opinion, October 23, 2023). This lack of faith in our form of government has caused many to believe that violence is justified to keep the other party from getting what it wants. Sadly, when people lose faith in their government, then we will see the rise of coercion and manipulation by those who are in power and want to hold on to that power no matter what.

This loss of faith in our system of government has caused some of those who have a public voice to trash the founding documents of our country. Eli Mystal, an MSNBC commenter, recently stated that the U.S. Constitution was not just bad, but it is actually trash, and we should get rid of it. He stated that we give too much deference to the Constitution that they believe it was written in stone by the finger of God. (SALON: Eli Mystal, "Our Constitution is trash, but the Supreme Court can be fixed," by Dean Obeidallah, March 23, 2022) This opinion comes from one who is considered to be a "Constitutional Scholar."

There are other examples of those who are in the legal profession and politics who speak critically of the Constitution and other founding documents. Harvard Law School professor said, "The Constitution Is Broken and Should Not Be Reclaimed" (HARVARD LAW SCHOOL FACULTY BIOGRAPHY: "The Constitution is Broken and does not need to be reclaimed," Ryan D. Doerfler of Harvard and Samuel Moyn, August 19, 2022)

The young adults coming out of the elite schools are coming out with not just questions about our democracy but are willing to consider another form of government system. These students are graduating with a dislike for America. Where schools in the past were established for the purpose of teaching patriotism and love for the country, schools today are filling the minds of students with the ideology of Marxism, Socialism, Critical Race Theory, and Diversity, Equity, and Inclusion. When they are taught these principles, they graduate with a negative attitude toward America.

Many of our politicians graduated from elite schools, and so now it should not be surprising what these elected officials are proposing. Some law professors are encouraging the President to ignore any Supreme Country ruling that he finds objectionable. Elizabeth Warren proposed that the number of Supreme Court Justices be expanded so more liberal justices can be put on the bench. Alexandria Ocasio Cortez questioned whether the Supreme

Court was even needed. Charles Schumer stood on the steps of the Supreme Court and threatened justices if they voted to overturn Roe V Wade. It is no wonder that a young man decided to travel to the home of Justice Kavenaugh for the purpose of killing him. These are just some of the statements that political leaders have made concerning the Constitution. (FOX NEWS OPINION; Jonathan Turley, "The greatest single threat to America is hiding in plain sight," October 23, 2023)

Sadly, every elected official is required to take an "Oath of Office" stating support of the Constitution. This is the oath every elected official is required to take. "I, ___, do solemnly swear (or affirm) that I will support and defend the Constitution of the United States against all enemies, foreign and domestic; that I will bear true faith and allegiance to the same; that I take this obligation freely, without any mental reservation or purpose of evasion; and that I will well and faithfully discharge the duties of the office on which I am about to enter. So, help me, God." (FEDERAL NEWS NETWORK, Jeffery Neal, January 4, 2021)

It appears that some determined that defending the Constitution meant either radically changing it, ignoring it if you don't like what it is saying, or just simply doing away with it.

Chapter 6: The Real Threat To America Is Spiritual

As stated above, American politics has always been divisive as men and women debate and hash out differences of opinion. Some of those negotiations can become quite brutal, and the exchanges can be even threatening. We have been fortunate as a country in that we have been able to work through our differences. We have been able to make some progress in the struggles we have. It is obvious that we still have a long way to go.

The political discourse of the past was different than it is today. In the past, there was no instant news. There was no video footage showing a debate or hearing what someone said. Now, we can see debate and argument when it is actually happening. We can hear people saying mean and angry things to each other. When those kinds of communications take place, those who are on the outside listening in begin to form opinions and even take sides. The political climate today has reached a critical point.

People are being fired from their jobs because of their political decisions or even their religious beliefs. Families are breaking up because of the political differences. People are fighting and rioting in the streets and on college campuses. Flash mobs attacked people just trying to enjoy a meal. Other groups have attempted to shame and humiliate others because of their political beliefs.

Not only are there political divisions, but there appears to be a moral and spiritual decline that is unprecedented.

The downward moral and spiritual direction of our nation is escalating. It is not just the Constitution and the founding documents that are being attacked, but the very framework of Faith is being challenged; marriage, the sanctity of life, stewardship of our material and financial resources, honesty, and integrity are no longer qualities that are considered admirable in people. Not only are political leaders and parties considered to be a threat to democracy, but so is the church. Yes, the church and the people of God are considered to be a serious threat to our society. This threat is so great that some elite leaders are calling for Christians to be removed from leadership roles in our society. One sitting senator said that he does not believe that practicing Christians need to be serving in government. "Senator Bernie Sanders doesn't think Christians are fit to serve in public office. In a shameful exchange, Sanders grilled Russell Vought, President Trump's nominee for Deputy Director of the White House Office of Management and Budget, about his Christian beliefs. When Vought refused to disavow his belief that Muslims "stand condemned" because "they have rejected Jesus Christ," Sanders became livid. "I would simply say, Mr. Chairman, that this nominee is really not someone who this country is supposed to be about," Sanders said. "I will vote no." (The Christian Post; Bernie Sanders thinks all Christians are disqualified from Public office." Julie Roys, July 8, 2017).

Senator Sen. **Dianne Feinstein** (D-Calif.), the ranking Democrat on the Judiciary Committee, told the nominee Amy Comey Barrett, who is Catholic, "The dogma lives loudly within you." (The Hill; Hawley warns Schumer to steer clear of Catholic-based criticisms of Barrett **ALEXANDER BOLTON** - 09/26/20)

The GOP senator Josh Hawley asserted that Senate Democrats "have attacked and attempted to disqualify nominees by questioning their views on the nature of sin, their beliefs about heaven and hell, their memberships in religious organizations, and the activities of their churches." "But our Constitution bans religious tests. Democrats ' offensive and wholly inappropriate attacks must not be repeated in this confirmation process," he wrote. (The Hill, Alexander Bolton, 9/26/20)

In a more troubling ruling, Christians are being singled out as unfit to be classroom teachers. "Effective July 2025, teacher licensing rules passed last year in Minnesota under Democrat Gov. Tim Walz will ban practicing Christians, Jews, and Muslims from teaching in public schools. Walz is now the presidential running mate of current U.S. Vice President Kamala Harris. Christians can be disqualified from teaching in Minnesota's public and even private schools if they do not affirm ideas that go against their beliefs. According to the National Review, starting next July, (2024). Minnesota agencies controlled by Walz appointees will require teacher license applicants to affirm transgenderism and race Marxism. Without a teaching license, individuals cannot work in Minnesota public schools or in the private schools that require such licenses. The latest version of the regulations requires teachers to "affirm" students" 'gender identity" and "sexual orientation" to receive a Minnesota teaching license: (THE FEDERALIST: "Under Tim Walz, Minnesota Banned Christians From Teaching In Public Schools" Joy Pullan, August 27, 2024).

These are just a few examples of not only a political decline but a moral and spiritual decline. However, there is an answer. The answer does not lie in Washington or any other government state house. The answer does not lie in our education because right now, our prestigious universities are teaching Marxism and Socialism to our students. The answer to the downward trend in America is the church.

The greatest threat to America is a disobedient and negligent church.

In my opinion, the greatest threat to America is the church failing to be who God called us to be and to do what God has asked us to do. Let's consider what our country needs from the church right now. I would suggest that our country needs the church to start being the church God intended it to be. We have been put here by God to give spiritual direction. We have been put here to be salt and light. We have been put here to point our society to the only moral compass that can bring peace, unity, and hope. That moral compass is Jesus. We are here to influence our world for good.

Today, because of the internet, Facebook, YouTube, and other social media outlets, a new group has been identified called influencers. These are people who influence society through their teachings, actions, political or religious statements, and personal interests. These men and women work to encourage followers to live a certain lifestyle or to be a person of change in our families or communities.

In reality, we, the church, are the true influencers of change. We are to influence people through our lives and testimonies to give their lives to Jesus and trust Him as their personal savior. We are to point men and women as the only ones who can heal the divide taking place in our country.

The only people who have been given the job to influence and change society is the church. God did not give the government that role. We are watching the inability of our political system to deal with the moral crisis around us. Sadly, our political divisions are exacerbating the problems, not helping. The government left to itself will only create more problems. It passes laws that are contradictory to the word of God. These laws also cause potential legal problems for Christians who refuse to violate their faith and their beliefs. That's why the government needs the influence and the spiritual help of the church. The founding fathers were very clear concerning the relationship of the church to the state. The Founders did not want the government to involve itself in the business of the church, but they expected the church to have an influence over the government.

Consider the promise God made to His people when they pray for their country.

When I shut up the heavens so that there is no rain, or command the locust to devour the land or send pestilence among my people, if my people who are called by my name humble themselves, and pray and seek my face and turn from their wicked ways, then I will hear from heaven and will forgive their sin and heal their land. (2 Chronicles 7:13-14)

This verse has been called the source and the direction for revival. If there are going to be any changes within our country from the political, educational, and social, then something has to happen to the church.

The first thing that we must do if we are going to affect the political and social climate in our country is to recognize who we are. We were the people of God. This passage begins with the phrase, '**If my people who are called by my**

name... 'These are the people who have a covenant relationship with God. These are those who called upon the Lord to save them from their sin. These are those who confessed that Jesus is the Son of God who died on the cross. They are those who believe in the resurrection of Jesus from the dead. And these are those who believe that Jesus is the only way to heaven.

This passage speaks about the kind of attention God gives His people. He is always aware of their situation and condition. He knows what they are going through. He is close to those who belong to Him. The good news is that God is waiting for his people to call on Him to meet their needs. In the context of this passage, God is waiting for His people to pray for their country. When we pray, He is listening to us and is ready to respond to us.

May we who are believers in Jesus recognize the power God has given us. He has given us the power to pray. He says pray for your country, and I will answer you.

Our praying for our country has conditions on it. We cannot live any way we want and expect God to answer us. No. He will answer us if we have the right spiritual attitude.

First, the members of the church need to humble themselves.

One of the problems that we face in our nation and in the life of the church is that we are too self-sufficient. We feel that we have everything we need and really don't need God to help us. It is interesting that God tells Solomon that the starting place for any revival or spiritual awakening is humility. We will not have any kind of spiritual awakening that does not have this as a component for the people of God.

This humility comes from one primary source it comes from God. What I mean by that is this: Humility comes when we have a true view of God. It comes when we see him for who he is.

1. We must see his majesty and glory

2. We must see his holiness.

3. We must see his goodness and mercy.

4. We must see him as all-powerful and all-knowing.

When this is our view of God, then humility is never a problem. But when we have the attitude of self-sufficiency, then we believe we have control over our lives and even over the events that happen in our lives. This kind of thinking is false, delusional thinking. We do not have control over our lives. Our lives are in the hands of God. He determines the length of our life and he also guides us through the experiences of our life. We do not have any control over whether or not we get sick. We don't have any control over events that happen. Once we understand that our life is totally dependent on God, then we will seek Him for help and we will pray for His intervention in our country.

The Second Thing We Must Do Is Pray.

The context of this verse talks about praying for our country. He is saying that He is listening to our prayers. He told us in His word that he is attentive to all of our prayers. Here He is talking about the prayers that we offer on behalf of our country. If we are concerned about the moral and social climate today, then we will be people who spend time praying for God's intervention for our land. He wants us to pray for those who are in the government. He wants us to pray for our leaders. At the same time, God wants us to pray for those who do not have a relationship with Him. He wants us to pray for those who have been victims of crimes. He wants us to pray for the immigrants, whether they are illegal or not. God wants us to pray for our own spiritual strength, asking Him to help us remain faithful in a very chaotic world.

We need to pray for the church and for those who believe in Christ. Sadly, there are fewer people claiming to be Christians today. Also, many churches have closed their doors because of a lack of attendance and support from Christians. We need to spend time praying that the people of God will experience a revival in their hearts and a desire to serve the Lord in these troublesome times.

We are to pray for the students on our college campuses. Many students who attend some of the most elite universities in our country are afraid to walk on campus or go to class because of the potential violence against them from protestors who are also on campus. We need to pray for university administrators that they will have the courage to deal with these protestors. Those who destroy property and threaten other students should lose their right to attend classes or be enrolled in school. Those who commit acts of violence against other students should be arrested and charged with assault. Sadly, with all of the protests going on, some protestors are being arrested but then immediately released without bail, only to return to the campus and continue distrusting the daily student activities.

We need to pray for our police officers. Since the death of George Floyd, police officers have come under attack. Some have been brutally ambushed and killed. Others have been attacked as they sit in their cars. Some have even been assaulted by violent gangs. Some of these assaults happen in public where everyone can see. These men serve in an institution created by God. God said in Romans 13 that those who serve in law enforcement are there for our good. They are there to protect us.

We need to pray for our children, with all of the gender ideology that is prevalent in some schools putting our children in danger of being misled about gender. Some schools refuse to inform parents if their child chooses to identify as another gender. We need to pray for Christian teachers who are threatened with the loss of their jobs if they don't follow or conform to school policy rules regarding gender. The schools in Minnesota passed a law that said that any teacher who refused to call a student by the name they chose or the gender they chose would be fired. They will not be able to teach. This law and others like it are a direct attack on the creative work of God. The Bible says that God created "male and female." He did not create any more than that. But there are those who attack one of the foundation principles of scripture when they deny that there are only two genders. This idea of gender identity has become so radical that even a student in school can be suspended if he claims that there are only two genders.

We need to pray for our cities and our local government. With the influx of illegal immigrants being spread across the country, most cities do not have the resources to take care of them. The federal government refuses to slow or stop the large number of people crossing the border to enter the U.S. Because of this influx, migrants are being sent to cities all across America. City governments are housing them, feeding them, and providing services for them. These cities are begging for help because their resources are limited. We need to pray that God will give wisdom to those who serve in local municipalities. May they be given the wisdom to deal with this immigration crisis.

We could go on and on listing various areas in which Christians need to pray. The point is that God is waiting for us to lift our voices to Him to ask for His power to be revealed through those who are serving in government.

As we pray for our country, we need to remember to pray for revival and spiritual awakening. But before we can ever pray like that, we have to believe that revival and spiritual awakening is needed. If we feel like, well, things could be better, but I don't think we have anything to worry about, then our prayer is not going to have the intensity it needs. My prayer is that each one of us and other Christians across our country will be so convicted of the spiritual need for revival and spiritual awakening that we will not let a day go by that we don't pray for it.

Let us pray that God will do something dramatic to bring us back to the place where we knew as a nation our dependence was on Him. Let us pray that God will bring us back to the place where His word becomes the rule of life for us.

We Must Seek His Face

To seek the face of God means to have a deep desire to know Him. To know Him means more than just knowing basic information. We are to seek His love and forgiveness for our sins. We are to seek His power and ask Him to bring about a revival in our country. One of the consequences of a prayer life is that we get to know God in a special and intimate way. We get to feel His presence. The more we know Him, the stronger we become in our faith. And, most important is that the more we know Him, the more like Him we become.

As we stated, the more intimate we are in prayer with God, the more we sense His presence. Along with sensing His presence, we also sense His pleasure. The movie "Chariots of Fire" is a story about a Scottish Athlete named Eric Liddell. He was a sprinter who won a spot on the British Olympic team. He had a sister who did not approve of His running. She felt that it took his focus off of his calling. In one scene in the movie, Eric is responding to his sister's complaint by saying, "When I run, I feel His pleasure." How could Eric Liddell say that? He could say that because of the intimate time, He spent with the Lord. He sensed the presence of God in his life and also God's pleasure in his life.

What a great statement. It is great to know God's presence, but even more wonderful to know His pleasure. This sense of His presence and His pleasure comes when we seek His face. Seeking His face means that we are not satisfied with what we know about the Lord. We want to know more.

In verse 13, God reveals some things about himself. He says that He is the one who is able to shut up the heavens where there is no rain. He is the one who has the power to cause a drought to come on the land. He is the one who can send a plague of locusts to devour all of the crops of the land. He is the one who can send a plague or a disease that can take the lives of people.

He describes himself as the powerful, almighty God who can do these things and more. And here he gives us an invitation to get to know him. When we read through the scriptures, we find that those men and women who did great things for God did not seek to do great things; they sought God.

When Moses was on the Mountain, he said to the Lord, LET ME SEE YOUR FACE.

When Isaiah was grieving over the loss of a friend, he said, I SAW THE LORD; HE WAS HIGH AND LIFTED UP.

When Paul was going through his missionary journeys, winning people to Christ and writing letters to the churches, he only had one primary desire: TO KNOW CHRIST AND THE POWER OF HIS RESURRECTION.

When the apostle John was on the island of Patmos about to die, he wrote I SAW THE LORD. He said that he had a voice like thunder. He was filled with glory that he shone like the sun. The presence of God was so great that John says I feel at his feet as though he were dead.

God says SEEK ME. Seek me when you are troubled, and it seems that everything is crashing down on you.

Seek me when the world is going crazy, and sin is rampant.

Seek me when you lose someone you love.

Seek me when you are sick and hurting.

Seek me when there is social and political unrest.

The point that God is making here is that THERE IS NO SATISFYING SOLUTION TO ANYTHING EXCEPT IN HIM.

If we are serious about the need for revival and spiritual awakening, if we are serious about the direction we are going as a nation, and if we realize the spiritual condition that we are in, then we must seek the face of God. The more that we know Him, the better we are going to be able to represent Him in the world. The more that we know Him, the more confident we will live as believers.

We must turn from our wicked ways: We must repent.

There are two important things we need to understand about this phrase. Repentance is a word which means to turn around. It means that we are going one way, and then we realize that we are going the wrong way, so we turn around to go the right way. This means that if we are doing those things that are not pleasing to the Lord, then we are to stop doing them, turn away from them, and start doing those things that are right.

The Bible is full of references to repentance. Now remember, this verse is to the people of God. This is for those who say that they are believers. So God is telling believers: REPENT FROM YOUR WICKED WAYS. Let's look at some of the things God says about repentance.

God Gives Us Time To Repent.

Rev. 2:21 says: "**I have given her time to repent of her immorality**." This is a verse that speaks to the sinfulness in a church. God is gracious in that He gives time for the people of God to repent of their sins so he can do the work that he wants to do. We know, according to the Word of God, that God wants to bring revival. He wants spiritual awakening to take place. But in order for Him to do these things, He needs His church to be in the right relationship with Him. The first thing we must do is examine our hearts, and if there are things in our lives that don't need to be there, then we must repent of those things.

Rev. 2:5 Consider how far you have fallen; repent and do the things you did at first. God is saying to look back at your life when you first became a Christian. Look at how you felt. Look at all of the desires you had to serve God, to praise God, and to live for him the very best that you could.

Now look at your life now. Is that same desire to serve God still there? Is that same love for Him still burning and driving your life? If that same desire to be fully committed to Him is still there. If it is not then the Lord says, remember those times. Go back to those times. Start doing the things that you did at the beginning, and when you do, you will be blessed by God, and He will be able to use you to bring about revival.

Job 42:6 says, **Therefore I despise myself and repent in dust and ashes**. Job understood what his sin was. He understood that sin in his life was not to be taken lightly. When he realized the sinfulness of his life, he loathed what it did. He said I despise myself for doing anything that would dishonor the Lord.

If there is ever going to be genuine revival and spiritual awakening in our land, then Christians are going to have to see the reality of sin and what it is. Every believer needs to have the same attitude toward sin that Job had. When we sin, no matter how small or how private, there needs to be an absolute hatred for what we have done. We need to grieve over the fact that we have wounded the heart of God. We need to grieve that we have added to the suffering of Jesus on the cross. There needs to be a loathing that we, who are called the children of God, would do anything like that.

But we cannot have that attitude of hatred toward sin if we do not take sin seriously. God says to Solomon that the people must turn from their WICKED WAYS. According to this verse and other verses, Sin is wickedness. We cannot take our sins lightly. If we look at sin as just some kind of mistake and some kind of oversight, then we are never going to see the seriousness of it. We must realize that all sin, no matter how small or large, is wicked and evil. When we have this attitude, then we will do what we can to get rid of it.

The question that we must answer is how badly we want revival and spiritual awakening. If we really desire it. If we really see the need for it, then we are going to follow these commandments to get it.

Yes, our country is in desperate shape right now. More and more, there is the celebration of wrong. There is the cheering of those things that are opposed to the word of God. Let us seriously pray for God to move in a mighty way in our nation.

God's Promises When We Obey Him

This is a wonderful passage because it reveals that when God's people do what God instructs them to do, He rewards them with His presence and with answered prayers. When we repent, seek His face, and humble ourselves, then God makes three wonderful promises.

I will hear from heaven.

As a dad of two daughters, I have to admit that there have been times when I was not attentive to the conversations my children had with me. I was either reading or watching TV but was not really listening. My youngest daughter knew when I was not paying attention. She could see if I was focused on something else. That did not deter her from getting my attention. During one of those times when I was not paying much attention to what was being said, she put her hands on my face and said, "Daddy, listen to me with your eyes." It was one of those moments when a young child pointed out the importance of paying attention when someone speaks to you.

The good news is that we don't have to negotiate for the attention of God. All we have to do is to begin our prayers with "Our Father who is in heaven." He is listening. He hears us.

One of the most iconic scenes from the tragic aftermath of 9/11 is when President George Bush stood on the rubble with a megaphone in his hand, making comments to those men who were working through the rubble to find survivors. When he was speaking, one of the men in the crowd shouted out, "We can't hear you." The president's response was, "I can hear you, and the ones who tore down these buildings will hear you as well."

That moment is very similar to the prayer life of believers. There are those times when we feel that our prayers are not getting through. There are those moments when it seems that God is not paying attention. We can't feel his presence. We are not sure if He is paying attention. In this verse, the Lord answers that question. He is letting us know that it does not matter what the circumstances are, how much noise or distractions are around you, or what kind of state of mind you are in. He says that when we pray, He will hear from heaven. What a great verse. Our Father is always attentive. He is always listening. So whenever you have something weighing on your mind and heart, just remember that God is listening and wants to hear what you have to say.

I Will Forgive Their Sin.

This is the second promise the Lord makes to those of us who turn to Him and seek Him. He promises that when we repent, He will forgive us. God's forgiveness is a remarkable experience. It is the kind of forgiveness that we cannot give to another person. Consider what I mean by that. When I sin against someone, I may repent and then ask them to forgive me. They may do that. They may forgive me for the offense I caused them.

However, even though they may forgive me, they will not forget what I did. They may not ever bring it up, but my sin is close to their minds. They remember. But God does not remember. This is one of the most remarkable things about the forgiveness of God. When God forgives us, He forgets about our sins. I don't know how that is possible, but He literally wipes our forgiven sins from His memory. The Bible says that all of our sins (that is, the sins of believers) are covered by the blood of Jesus. When God looks at us, He does not see a sinner doomed for hell, but he sees a child of God who is going to spend eternity with Him in heaven. What a great gift God gives us every day: THE GIFT OF FORGIVENESS.

I Will Heal Their Land.

The healing of the land is a reference to the moral and sinful behavior of the people. Consider the kind of healing that we need today.

We need healing from our gender disobedience. God created male and female. Those who claim that there are more than two genders are being disingenuous. Scientifically, the physiology of men and women is different. The way men and women respond to problems is different. We have new kinds of experts today who say that gender is not biological but is mental and emotional. So, if I get up in the morning and decide that I am not a man today, but I am a woman, nothing has changed in me physically. The only thing that changed is how I think of myself.

The reason these so-called experts are saying that there is more than one gender is because they are thinking with an unspiritual and carnal mind. Romans 1:21 says:

For although they knew God, they did not honor him as God or give thanks to him, but they became futile in their thinking, and their foolish hearts were darkened. Claiming to be wise, they became fools. (ESV).

Notice that the way men think about the world depends on what they think about God. Paul says that when someone does not honor God, they become vain in their thinking. (KJV) "Become vain," means to be elated, or to be self-conceited, or to seek praise from others. The meaning here seems to be that they became foolish and frivolous in their thoughts and reasonings. They acted foolishly; they employed themselves in useless and frivolous questions, the effect of which was to lead the mind further and further from the truth respecting God. (Barnes Commentary on Romans; Romans 1:21-22)

The ESV says that they became futile in their thinking. The word used here means empty, useless, or worthless. This is God's description of those who determine that God's word is not relevant to the issues of the day. They create all kinds of foolish ideas that many in the population accept as truth when it is nothing more than a lie. It is a lie that there are more than two genders. It is a lie that a person can change their biology. Yes, they can have surgical procedures, but that does not change the truth of who they are.

The foolish thinking comes when there are those who identify as some kind of animal. One lady wore cat ears every day, claiming that she identified as a cat. My granddaughter, who attends an art university, told me that there are students in her school who identify themselves as "furries." These are students to think that they are some kind of animal. They might claim to be a cat, dog, beaver, parakeet, or any other kind of animal. According to the scripture, I think this could be classified as foolish, useless, and empty thinking.

It is the kind of thinking that directly contradicts what God says in His word. It is a belief that denies the truth of God's word. Those who feel the need to change their identity. There are those who have been convinced that God made a mistake with them. If they are a man and think they should be a woman, then they are confessing that God made a mistake. If God makes a mistake, then that means God is not perfect, and since He is not perfect, there is no need to obey Him or believe Him.

Paul concludes this verse with the phrase, "**They became fools**." These are those men and women who believe they are the smartest people in the room. They consider themselves so wise because they supposedly think outside the box. God's Word says that those who have these useless, empty thoughts are fools. Why would Paul call them this? It is because these "wise" people really don't believe in God. If they do believe in God, it is not the God of the Bible. They believe in a God that accommodates their futile thinking. The Bible clearly states, "The fool has said in his heart, there is no God." These useless, ridiculous thoughts give an indication that they do not really believe in God because their thoughts and beliefs are so contradictory to God's Word.

Paul goes on to describe these men and women as having foolish hearts that are darkened. There is no internal light to guide them. These are the blind guides of the day. These are the ones who determine what kinds of subjects need to be taught in school. These are the ones who say that Christian men and women do not need to be teachers, politicians, or anyone who has influence in society.

These are examples of the kind of healing that we need in our nation. If we, the people of God, "turn from our wicked ways, humble ourselves, and seek the face of God, He will heal our land." Let us take seriously the spiritual condition around us and recognize that the only way any of this is going to change is through the move of God on the hearts of His children. May we pray for and seek that change.

Chapter 7: The Battle Over Gender

Over the past two years, the defiance of God has grown worse. One of the prominent attacks on the authority and the creation of God is the subject of gender. I never believed that I would live in a time where there was such a blatant disregard for the authority of God as well as the rejection of the word of God. These attacks have to do with the most ridiculous ideas in modern times. We now have those who are in our school systems encouraging children to question their gender. This is a blatant rejection of God's creation.

Genesis 2:21-25 says:

So the LORD God caused a deep sleep to fall upon the man, and while he slept took one of his ribs and closed up its place with flesh. And the rib that the LORD God had taken from the man he made into a woman and brought her to the man. Then the man said, "This at last is bone of my bones and flesh of my flesh; she shall be called Woman, because she was taken out of Man." Therefore, a man shall leave his father and his mother and hold fast to his wife, and they shall become one flesh. And the man and his wife were both naked and were not ashamed. (ESV)

The modern ideology rejects this truth. The so-called experts say there are as many as 35 genders, and even more are being identified. Some are claiming to be no particular gender. They claim to be binary, neither male nor female. According to these ideologues, God made mistakes, and He is still making mistakes. Because they believe God made mistakes, then, they assume that most children being born today are misgendered. As they get older, they are told they can change their gender. They are lied to early in their life.

We are now in the savage times of abusing and mutilating children. That's bad, but what's worse, this mutilation has government approval. Let's look at some recent policies that show that the government, education, and social services are opposing calling children by their gender.

The Vermont Department of Health

According to a report on FOX News, the Vermont Department of Health is advising educators and families to change how they refer to their children. The department suggests that parents and educators no longer call their children sons and daughters when speaking about their children or addressing them in the classroom. The so-called professionals feel that changing the language of how we address children will change the way they respond in society. They are saying that the term son or daughter needs to be removed and replaced with gender-neutral words. (Fox News Media, Aubrey Spady, August 24, 2024)

Can you imagine how even more confusing it would be for young children who are not called by their proper pronoun of son or daughter? In my own personal opinion, this opens the door for other so-called professionals to encourage children to make a sex change, even when they do not feel they need to. Those who are promoting this ideology believe that somehow, this gender-neutral language helps the child to achieve equity as they become adults. Not only is this a danger to the emotional and psychological well-being of the child, it is another blatant attack on the authority of the family.

According to some historians, the building blocks of America were the family, the church, and education. The founding fathers considered the family to be the primary and most important relationship that anyone could have. These men also believe that the church was the founding principle in the beginning and the development of America. The writers of the Declaration of Independence and the Constitution referred to the fact that the rights we have do not come from government but they are the inalienable rights that come from God. The third level of the foundation was education. The founders believed that Americans needed to have a good education to be good Americans. The primary subjects taught in universities were history, Latin, Bible, Math, and English. The founders believed that those who moved in from other countries needed to be taught about America. They needed to know about American laws, history, and government. The founders intended that these subjects would make the newcomers patriots.

So here we are in 2024, seeing everything the founders fought to for being challenged. Students are graduating without a love for the country. It is no longer unusual for some college professors to be heard saying that the Constitution is a useless document and America needs to be torn down and rebuilt. Some of those believe that America needs to be torn down because we have not yet paid for our past sins, such as slavery.

Three policies were proposed to help students feel included and not left out because they may not be the son or daughter of the family they are living with. They may be a foster child or an orphan who does not have parents. The second policy suggestion is to say "family members" rather than "household members" because not all family members live in the same house. Some children live in a blended family with step-parents, while their biological parents may live elsewhere. And the third suggestion is to say "family" rather than "extended family," which could include grandparents, aunts, and uncles who live elsewhere.

The state's health department promotes a "health equity glossary" involving similar rhetoric on its website. The glossary, reviewed by Fox News Digital, defines gender as "social, psychological, and/or emotional traits, often influenced by societal expectations, that classify someone as man, woman, a mixture of both, or neither" and says it is "socially constructed." (FOX NEWS: Vermont encourages everyone to replace "sons and daughters" with gender-neutral terms in school." Aubrey Spady, August 29, 2024)

Student Expelled And Arrested For Saying There Are Only Two Genders

A sixth-grade student was disciplined and suspended from school for saying, GOD CREATED A MAN AND A WOMAN; THERE ARE ONLY TWO GENDERS. Josh Alexander was suspended last November over comments made about gender in class and told he couldn't return to class until he recanted. A lawyer representing Alexander said that the school wouldn't let him attend classes again until he agrees "not to use the 'dead name' of any transgender student and agreed to exclude himself from his afternoon classes because those classes are attended by two transgender students who disapprove of Josh's religious beliefs." (The "dead name" is the students birth name) When Josh returned to school, he was arrested for trespassing. (TORONTO SUN: "High School student suspended and arrested for saying there are only two genders," Brian Lilly, February 8, 2023).

The sad thing about this story is that it is a Catholic School that is either rejecting or refusing to teach Catholic doctrine to students. The school administration and teachers are defying their own beliefs by teaching about multiple genders. The policy of the school is to recognize any gender identification a student has. The number of genders is only limited to the number of identifications a student may have. It can be an unlimited number. (Alliance Defending Freedom: Faith and Justice," Teed Off, A school tries to silence a quiet objection to gender, Chris Potts, February 2, 2023)

After reading this report, I was reminded of a sermon I heard when I was in seminary. Dr. Eddie Lieberman was a Jewish evangelist. He was a brilliant preacher. In this particular sermon, he was referencing how liberal some of our seminaries were becoming. His comment is worth considering today. He said that "some people were so open-minded that their brains were falling out." (Sermon preached by Eddie Lieberman at Texas Baptist Evangelism Conference, January 1976) The open-mindedness of politicians, educators, bureaucrats, and even some religious leaders is setting policies that have the potential of destroying families. The purpose of all these policies is to remove the authority of parents to raise their children according to their values and beliefs. If a parent promotes Christian values in the home, some officials feel that is a threat to the well-being of the students.

A Christian student is expected to attend school and be silent on all of the cultural and social policies that go against his beliefs. In Josh Alexander's appeal to the school board, he commented that he sees a lot of things that he does not agree with. He sees gay pride flags and gay pride days. He sees trans students who are boys and yet wear dresses. His computer and laptop were taken away and all items that had to do with gender were removed from his platform. It became obvious that transgender students' rights trump the rights of those who do not agree with them.

Massachusetts Removes Father And Mother From State Birth Certificates.

Massachusetts state government has passed a bill that removes the words father and mother from its birth certificates and replaces them with "person" and 'person who gave birth. 'It is not willing to recognize parents as men and women. This is the next step in the attack on the family. Some state laws remove the word woman from the language of their bills. Looks like more and more people either do not know or choose to reject the pronoun woman. We even have a Supreme Court justice who cannot define what a woman is. So, it is only natural to remove the pronouns of the traditional family and replace them with neutral language. Removing traditional pronouns from the family makes it easier for a liberal, ungodly government to remove children from the homes of parents they deem a danger to children. In reality, the dangerous ones are those who pass laws like this.

All of this craziness is an attack on the traditional family but also an attack on Christians who use the Bible to determine who a parent is. The Bible is very clear that the parents of children are mothers and fathers. When you reject the Bible as the guide for life, you come up with some of the most ridiculous actions. This is just one of many. Sadly it shows how far we have fallen when we reject the Word of God as our guide and instruction book for our lives.

This is only going to get worse. The only way we are going to get back to some kind of normalcy is for God to intervene and change the hearts and minds of men and women who are making these ridiculous decisions. May we pray that God will bring a spiritual awakening to our country.

The Massachusetts state's health department promotes a "health equity glossary" involving similar rhetoric on its website. The glossary, reviewed by Fox News Digital, defines gender as "social, psychological, and/or emotional traits, often influenced by societal expectations, that classify someone as man, woman, a mixture of both, or neither" and says it is "socially constructed." (FOX NEWS: Vermont encourages everyone to replace "sons and daughters" with gender-neutral terms in school." Aubrey Spady, August 29, 2024)

Washington Teacher Believes That Christian Parents Are A Threat To Students.

A Washington teacher believes that schools have the right and also the responsibility to keep students' information private from parents. Karen Love states that she believes that Christian parents are the problem. She calls these parents Christo-fascists. She believes and promotes the idea that Christian parents are responsible for the racist behavior of their students. She believes that Christians promote white supremacy. She makes this claim because there are so many "white" teachers in the public schools, and these white teachers promote racism using their Christian beliefs. Because she believes that Christian parents are a threat to students, then the school has the right to refuse to give private information about students to the parents. (FOX NEWS: Washington teacher says schools must do more to keep student info from Christo-fascist parents, Joshua Nelson, February 28, 2023)

Chapter 8: Filling The Void With DEI And CRT

How did we get to the point where Christian beliefs are considered to be inappropriate for students to learn and practice? How did Christians become the enemies of education? How did we reach the time when Christian students are being targeted because they do not agree with these liberal and un-Christian themes? I believe the answer is found in the word of God.

Suppose we consider that over the past several decades, the war against Christianity has been playing out in the courts. Since the beginning of public education in American, there was always time for prayer and Bible Study. Prior to 1962 prayer and Bible readings were a part of the daily routine for public schools. In 1962 the Supreme Court ruled that schools were forbidden to read or quote prayers that were written by school officials or others. The ruling by the court stated that students could pray privately, and they could also engage in personal religious training time during the school day as long as that training is off-campus. This ruling is still in place. Students can pray as long as they initiate the prayer. Teachers and administrators are forbidden to participate or lead in these prayer times.

Since 1962, there has been a concerted effort not just to remove prayer from school but anything that has to do with Christianity. Through the years, the hostility toward Christians practicing their faith in school is constantly challenged. Some teachers have been reprimanded because they had a Bible on their desks. A high school coach lost his job because he would go to the 50-yard line at the end of every game, kneel down, and thank God that no one was hurt. Some players asked if they could join. He never encouraged them or invited them, but they wanted to be a part of what he was doing. Eventually, some complained about the violation of the "Separation Clause" preventing this kind of behavior. Soon, the coach was fired.

Education is not the only place where hostility to Christianity is found. This hostility is also found in the public square.

So, back to the question, how did we get here? Jesus told a parable that might answer this question.

Mathew 12:43-45. 43 **"When an impure spirit comes out of a person, it goes through arid places seeking rest and does not find it. 44 Then it says, 'I will return to the house I left.' When it arrives, it finds the house unoccupied, swept clean, and put in order. 45 Then it goes and takes with it seven other spirits more wicked than itself, and they go in and live there. And the final condition of that person is worse than the first. That is how it will be with this wicked generation."**

This is a great story for our generation. When we consider that Bible reading, prayer, and meditation have been removed from education, politics, culture, and social issues, it leaves a vacuum. Anytime there is an emptiness created, something has to fill it. Something has to replace what was removed. So, when the spiritual principles of life are removed, then those unspiritual principles and ideologies find a home. Since we are not going to have prayer in school anymore, let's replace it with transgenderism. The gender question and controversy attack the very act of creation. The book of Genesis says that God created man and woman. This statement of creation goes against the whole idea of transgenderism. Transgenderism means that we, humans, have the power to add other genders or change our gender if we choose to do so. We no longer have two genders, but we have a whole list of genders, and some have yet to be created. The radical transgender movement even allows men and women, boys and girls, to identify as something other than human. Some young people identify as furries. They dress up like cats, dogs, beavers, rabbits, squirrels, and other animals and claim that this is who they are. Thirty or forty years ago, this would have been considered a mental illness. But not today. Today, this is acceptable and approved thinking.

The vacuum is also filled with diversity, equity, and inclusion, which tries to create equity and diversity. This means that people are hired to do a job that they may not be able to do, but they get this job because equity requires that a certain number of women must be hired, a certain number of ethnic minorities must be given positions even if they are not qualified to hold those positions.

I notice that this only works in the world outside of sports. The sports world does not believe in equity or diversity. The sports world believes in talent. A person who plays on a team must have the talent and the ability to play that position. It would be ridiculous to place a three-hundred-pound lineman as a wide receiver or someone four feet tall to play professional basketball. There is no equity here; there is only talent and ability.

However, this does not fit the conversation today. Society and politics have moved away from talent to diversity and equity. This has caused some companies to lose business and has even put in danger some who serve in law enforcement.

Not only does DEI fill the void, but also CRT: Critical Race Theory. This is the idea that a person is who he or she is based on their race. According to CRT, if a person is white, they are always going to be a perpetrator of minority groups. And if a person is black, he or she is always going to be a victim. According to this doctrine, there is nothing you can do to change who you are, so you are either going to be guilty all of your life or a victim all of your life, even if you have done nothing to deserve that identification. It's not based on what you do. It's based on the color of your skin.

In the parable that Jesus told, he pointed out that when the demon returned to his former home, he invited his friends to come and join him. Jesus said that the return of the demon and his friends made things worse. This seems to be the case with our society today. Since we are rejecting Christian values, which show the importance and the value of the individual, we have accepted the devilish values that denigrate a person, attack a person, or even try to punish a person because of what they believe.

If you believe that there are two genders, then there is something wrong with you. If you believe that people need to be promoted based on talent and ability, then you are racist. None of these are true. We, as Christians, need to pray that those who belong to Christ and His church have the courage and the strength to stand and speak the truth. We need to pray that believers will have the courage of the disciples when they are on trial. Peter and John said, "We will obey God rather than men." May that phrase be the theme of our life.

Remember, though, that when we choose to obey God rather than follow the deceptions of the day, there are going to be consequences. We may have to pay a price, such as being fired from our job, getting expelled from school, and even being rejected by family. As bad as these experiences are, they are nothing compared to the experience we will have when we get to heaven. An old gospel song reminds us that "it will be worth it all when we see Jesus."

Chapter 9: The Hostility Toward The Basic Christian Doctrine

Jesus is God and is the only way to heaven.

From the moment the church was born, on the Day of Pentecost, it has been attacked because of its focus on the Lord Jesus Christ. The major doctrine of the church is focused on the person of Jesus. We believe that Jesus is the Son of God, who became a man for the purpose of saving us from our sins and giving us a new life. Jesus came to provide the doorway into the presence of God for all believers. It is through Jesus that eternal life is given. It is through Jesus that the blessing of the Holy Spirit is given. All of the blessings of the Christian life come through Jesus and Jesus alone. Finally, and most importantly, the church teaches that belief in Jesus as God's son is essential to have eternal life. It is the confession of Jesus as Lord that grants access to heaven.

In Romans 10:13-15 Paul says,

"If you confess with your mouth that Jesus is Lord and believe in your heart that God raised him from the dead, you will be saved. For with the heart, one believes and is justified, and with the mouth, one confesses and is saved. The Scripture says, "Everyone who believes in him will not be put to shame." (ESV)

Jesus said,

"I am the door. No man comes to the Father except through me." (John 14:6)

Romans 5:1 says,

"We have peace with God THROUGH THE LORD JESUS."

Ephesians 2:18 says,

"Through Him we have access to the Father."

There are many other verses of scripture we can refer to that continue to emphasize the point that Jesus is the God-Man, and there is no access to God without going through Him. There is no access to salvation outside of believing in Christ.

The world considers this theology and this belief that Jesus is the only way to heaven as a dangerous belief because it refuses to recognize the beliefs of other religions. The belief that Jesus is the only way to heaven is considered to be exclusionary. This means that if a person does not believe this about Jesus, then he can't go to heaven. Those who reject that truth about Jesus do not believe that God would not exclude someone from heaven just because he does not believe in Jesus. In the eyes of many in the world, Jesus is just one of many ways to get into heaven. Sadly, there are some pastors in Christian churches who teach this false doctrine that there are more ways to heaven than just going through Jesus.

According to *The Christian Post,* 70% of church members believe that there is more than one way to get to heaven. Jesus is not the only way. Nearly 70% of born-again Christians disagree with the biblical position that Jesus is the only way to God, according to a new survey from Probe Ministries, a nonprofit that seeks to help the Church renew the minds of believers with a Christian worldview. Over three thousand Christians were polled from all religious groups. 717 of the respondents identified as "born-again

Christians." These are people who stated that they made a personal commitment of their life to Jesus. These same respondents claimed that Jesus is very important in their life. They stated because they confessed their sins and accepted Jesus as their savior that, they are going to heaven (*The Christian Post:* Nearly 70% of Born-Again Christians believe that other religions can lead to heaven, Senior Reporter; Leonardo Blair, October 21, 2021)

How is that possible when Jesus Himself stated that He is the only way to heaven? Could it be that this heretical thinking is caused by what they are hearing from some pulpits today? Could it be that preachers are preaching this heresy in their sermons?

Another possibility is the influence of social media, Facebook, Instagram, and even TikTok. As this message of many ways to heaven is being repeated over and over again, believers who are not grounded in the Word of God are mislead by this false gospel. The Bible predicts that this happens in the church when the truth of who Jesus is not being preached. Paul said in 2 Corinthians 11:3,

But I am afraid that as the serpent deceived Eve by his cunning, your thoughts will be led astray from a sincere and pure devotion to Christ. (ESV)

Throughout history, the church has experienced all kinds of persecution, trials, tribulations, slander, and false teachings. Jesus warned us that this would come. The Bible teaches that Christians are going to be challenged on their theology, and their testimony about Jesus is the only way to heaven. Because of these attacks and challenges, each Christian should be able to defend their faith in Jesus. Peter challenged believers to have such a knowledge of the Word of God that they would be able to answer the questions anyone might have about our faith. Peter said, 1 Peter 3:15:

"In your hearts honor Christ the Lord as holy, always being prepared to make a defense to anyone who asks you for a reason for the hope that is in you; yet do it with gentleness and respect" (ESV).

Notice the phrase "always be prepared." Not only should we be prepared to defend our faith, but we must have confidence in what we believe about Jesus. We must not become anxious when some new teaching is revealed, or some archaeological find is made that seems to contradict the Bible or add to it.

I remember several years ago, an article came out in various news articles about how someone found an artifact that had "The Gospel of Thomas" in it. When that article came out, I had many people calling asking for an appointment to talk about what they were reading. They needed clarification that this was a false gospel. They also needed to learn that this was not a new find. It had been in existence for hundreds of years. Yet, these Christians were worried that all they believed was not complete.

This kind of anxiety reveals that some believers don't have a deep level of confidence in their faith. When a false story comes out, they get worried. This worry or anxiety comes from a lack of knowledge and depth of understanding of the Word of God. It is an indication that many believers get their information through attending church and listening to sermons. However, attendance is good and needed, but just hearing a sermon on Sunday without any follow-up study and reading does not prepare us to defend our faith. The defense of our faith comes through study and meditation of the word. It comes from putting the word of God in our minds. Just one 30-minute sermon does not prepare us to face the intellectual challenges of the world. We must spend time learning how to defend the very essence of our faith which says that Jesus is God in the flesh and His death on the cross provides the only way to salvation.

The Hostility Toward Christians Who Practice Their Faith

It seems that the attitude of society is that it is okay for Christians to practice their faith in church, but they are not to practice their faith outside the walls of the church building. It is one thing to have hostility toward the doctrines and the theology of the church, but it is another thing to be hostile to those who are actually living and speaking out what they believe.

Over the past several years, members of the Christian Community have been attacked for their faith and their belief in Jesus. There are so many examples of this hostility toward Christians that we would not have time to list every example. But there are some examples that have gained worldwide attention. Below are just some of these examples.

A school teacher was dismissed from her class because she posted something on Facebook about her faith.

A primary school teacher in Gloucestershire, England, expressed her concerns about a "Relationship Curriculum" being taught to her son." The church school dismissed her for "Gross Misconduct." When I hear the phrase "gross misconduct," I think of something that would be so disgusting that people would turn away from it and not want to see it or be around it. That was not the case here. The gross misconduct was the sharing of her faith and how her faith cannot support the curriculum being taught. As a Christian, she did not want her son to learn about LGBT relationships.

The school administration responded and said that she was not fired for her faith. The administration claimed the wording she used in her posts that was considered to be hate speech. Because it was deemed hate speech, she was terminated. We are living in a time when there is disagreement over a subject, policy, or law, and disagreement can be considered either hate speech or racist speech. (We will address the race issue later.) The courts determined that the school had the right to dismiss her. In a statement made outside the courthouse, she said, "I am not alone in this." Many other Christians have been disciplined, fired, or dismissed from their positions because of their Christian faith. She went on to say that it cannot be right that so many Christians are losing their jobs because of their Christian belief. (NewsBreak.com; THE INDEPENDENT: Christian teacher sacked for online post saying she is not alone. Callum Parke, October 2, 2024)

Christian Man Fined And Arrested For Silently Praying Near An Abortion Clinic

Sebastian Vaughan-Spruce, a 44-year-old landscape gardener and pro-life activist, was fined on May 16 in Birmingham, England, over suspicion of his silent thoughts in violation of a "buffer zone code." He carried no sign and remained completely silent until approached by officers, in which he clarified he was not <u>praying silently</u> in his head. Police officers asked Vaughan-Spruce if he was "praying for the lives of unborn children" when he was found standing on a public street <u>near the abortion facility</u> in Kings Norton, Birmingham. When he asked officers what his alleged crime was, they asked him to move elsewhere. "Others were present there at the same time, yet I was singled out because of the beliefs I happen to hold," he said. (FOXNEWS.COM; Man fined for standing silently across from an abortion clinic, and the officers could not tell him what his crime was. Writer Kendal Tietz, May 25, 2024)

The British government passed a law setting up buffer zones in certain spaces. These buffer zones were implemented by the authorities, which criminalize individuals perceived to be engaging in any act of approval or disapproval in relation to abortion, including through verbal or written means, prayer, or counseling. It seems that we have now arrived at what the book 1984 predicted. People can be arrested, charged, jailed, and fined just for their thoughts. So, if a Christian is praying silently, not holding a sign, or interfering with someone wanting to go into the abortion clinic, he or she can be fined and even arrested just for the thoughts they have, (FOXNEWS.COM, May 24, 2024)

Bible College Fires Theologian And Threatens To Report Him As A Terrorist To The Police

I wish this story was some kind of outlier or just an anomaly in reporting, but sadly, this is not. This story has so many layers of hypocrisy, false doctrine, and a rejection of the word of God. A Methodist Bible college in the U.K. fired a Christian theologian and threatened to report him as a terrorist because of his tweets in opposition to homosexuality, his attorneys claimed.

Dr. Aaron Edwards, who taught theology at Cliff College in Derbyshire, England, was dismissed from the

91

school after being accused of "bringing the college into disrepute" on social media.

"Homosexuality Is Invading The Church."

Edwards tweeted on Feb. 19: "Evangelicals no longer see the severity of this [because] they're busy apologizing for their apparently barbaric homophobia, whether or not it's true." This *is* a 'Gospel issue, by the way. If sin is no longer sin, we no longer need a Savior.

The tweet went viral and prompted blowback, to which Edwards responded: "That *is* the conservative view. The acceptance of homosexuality as 'not sinful' *is* an invasion upon the Church, doctrinally. This is not controversial. The acceptance is controversial. Most of the global Church would agree. It is not homophobic to declare homosexuality sinful."

Edwards' tweets reportedly caused "distress" among members of the Methodist Church in Britain, with one senior staff member saying they "could be extremely damaging" and "impact the college's core work" and "business plan," according to Edwards' legal counsel at the London-based Christian Legal Centre.

Edwards was suspended from the school pending an investigation, and the college revealed during a disciplinary hearing on March 8 that it was considering referring him to prevent, which makes allegations of terrorism in the U.K. (FOXNEWS.COM. *Collage fires theologian for his tweet against homosexuality: Jon Brown (Fox News Reporter) March 19, 2023)*

The Methodist church has been in a theological struggle over the issue of homosexuality and same-sex marriage.

Thousands of churches have left the congregation to join together to create a conservative Methodist Church that teaches and upholds scripture. A teaching or a theological practice that refuses to call sin for what it is a church that has lost its mission, which is to proclaim the truth of the gospel. Churches are not given the right to pick and choose which scriptures they are going to teach. They are called upon to teach the entire word of God. It is one thing to be attacked by the world that does not know Christ or His word and yet another thing to be attacked by the church you are a member of because that church refuses to believe the totality of the word of God.

In the book of Revelation, Jesus writes a letter to seven churches. He compliments these churches on the work they are doing, but at the same time, he speaks to problems in the church.

To the church in Ephesus, he says, I **have this against you. YOU HAVE LEFT YOUR FIRST LOVE**. (Revelation 2:4)

To the church in Smyrna, he writes, **I know your tribulation and your poverty (but you are rich) and the slander of those who say that they are Jews and are not but are a synagogue of Satan**. (Revelation 2:9). Jesus was warning them of the false teachers who are in the church. He said these false teachers come from Satan himself. He sent his minions into the church to teach lies and they were deceiving the church. This statement can refer to those of the Methodist denomination or any other religious denomination that refuses to stand by the truth of the gospel when it comes to relationships. The false teachers at Smyrna were adding to the gospel. They were saying that salvation by faith in Jesus is not enough. There are other rites and traditions you must go through in order to be saved. The truth of the gospel is that Jesus is enough for salvation. Nothing else is needed.

The false teaching of the Methodist church is not adding to the gospel, but taking away from it. In the case of homosexuality, the Bible is very clear. It is considered sinful behavior. This does not mean that homosexuality is a sin worse than other sins. It is not. Neither does it mean that God hates homosexuals. He loves them in the same way he loves all people. The passage of scripture in Romans 8 that says **there is nothing that can separate us from the love of God means what it says.**

The false teaching in the Methodist church is that it refuses to accept the word of God when it comes to relationships. Those who listen to these false teachings and others like them are getting a distorted gospel. That distorted gospel causes confusion and sometimes even rejection of the gospel.

Jesus then sends a letter to the church in Pergamum. The church was experiencing some of the same problems that the church in Smyrna had. The church in Pergamum had false teachers who were leading the church away from the truth. In Revelation 2:14-16: He says, **But I have a few things against you: you have some there who hold the teaching of Balaam, who taught Balak to put a stumbling block before the sons of Israel so that they might eat food sacrificed to idols and practice sexual immorality. So also you have some who hold the teaching of the Nicolaitans. Therefore repent. If not, I will come to you soon and war against them with the sword of my mouth.** These false teachers were leading the church into immorality. They were claiming that a person could be a Christian and at the same time have other beliefs as well. They also taught that sexual immorality was not a problem. It was just part of how people lived, and the church could accept that.

Jesus shows how seriously he takes these false teachers and the doctrines they espouse. He says that if the church does not repent from these beliefs and stop listening to these false teachers, He will come and war against them. The idea presented here is that if the Son of God goes to war against you, the results are pre-determined. You will lose, and the outcome will be devastating.

To each of these churches, Jesus stated that their primary mission was to worship Him and then serve Him in the world. They were not to change the truth of the gospel. They were not to add other unnecessary acts or rites to the salvation Jesus offered. They were not to get caught up idolatry. Jesus was to be the exclusive love of our life.

When the church does not proclaim the truth of the gospel, then those who are members of those churches will be living under a lie rather than the truth. When those who are called Christians start living a lie rather than the truth, as we have seen will become hostile and antagonistic to those who are trying to live by what Jesus said. Those who live under a lie will accept the theology of the world, which is a complete contradiction to His Word.

All of the churches identified in Revelation were warned about false teachers and false doctrines. False doctrines do not give people stability. It makes them question the truth. It makes them willing to attack other Christians who do not believe as they do.

The attacks on the church and church members are increasing. Some of the attacks are violent and disruptive.

Over the past two years, churches and synagogues have been vandalized because of the overturn of the Roe v Wade. Some have even disrupted church services to express their hatred of the people of God.

It has been reported that one man has gone into churches during worship services to verbally attack the pastor or priest. Sebastian Church in Ross Township is one of the 10 churches that the man allegedly walked into to yell at a priest during Mass. In a statement, the Diocese of Pittsburgh said the man got in the priest's face and yelled that he was the devil on April 17. (CBSNEWS.COM, "Man accused of yelling at priest and calling him the devil, Shirley Bortz, April 25, 2024)

Several women attended the worship service led by Joel Olsteen and stripped down to their underwear to protest the church's stance against abortion. (INDY100.COM, Abortion activists strip down during Joel Olsteen sermon, Brianna Robinson June 7, 2022)

I know that these are disturbing videos to see and difficult to read about, but we, as Christians, should not be surprised when these things happen. Jesus said we should expect to be persecuted and experience hostility from the world. He said, **in the world, you will have tribulation, but don't be afraid, for I have overcome the world. (John 16:33, ESV)**. Jesus also said that those who are believers will be hated by the world. The reason we will be hated is because the world hated Him.

According to the scripture, this kind of hostility and hatred is not going to get better. They are going to get worse. Believers must prepare for this hostility by spending time in prayer and communion with the Father. We can prepare by putting on the armor of God. In Ephesians, Paul speaks about the kind of armor we need. It is the armor that fights against spiritual darkness and false teaching and gives us the courage and the ability to face the attacks that come against us and all those who have faith in Jesus.

Finally, be strong in the Lord and in the strength of his might. Put on the whole armor of God so that you may be able to stand against the schemes of the devil. For we do not wrestle against flesh and blood, but against the rulers, against the authorities, against the cosmic powers over this present darkness, against the spiritual forces of evil in the heavenly places. Therefore take up the whole armor of God, that you may be able to withstand in the evil day, and having done all, to stand firm. Stand therefore, having fastened on the belt of truth, and having put on the breastplate of righteousness, and, as shoes for your feet, having put on the readiness given by the gospel of peace. In all circumstances, take up the shield of faith, with which you can extinguish all the flaming darts of the evil one; and take the helmet of salvation, and the sword of the Spirit, which is the word of God, praying at all times in the Spirit, with all prayer and supplication. To that end, keep alert with all perseverance, making supplication for all the saints. (Ephesians 5;10-18)

Chapter 10: The Savage Abuse And Mutilation Of Children

One of the most disturbing trends and policies of our time has to do with gender. I understand that there are adults who wrestle with the feeling that they are in the wrong body and, after a lot of thought and counsel, decide to go through a gender change procedure. I also understand that for an adult to make that decision, they must have gone through a life of psychological pain as they felt out of place in their own body. I may not agree with the gender change that some make, but it is not up to me to pass judgment on those who make this decision. I know that those who make that decision have been judged and criticized by others. Some of the most damming criticism has come from Christians. I think that it is very important for those who are Christians to remember a wonderful verse in Romans where Paul says,

"Who shall separate us from the Love of Christ? Shall tribulation, or distress, or persecution, or famine, or nakedness, or danger, or sword? As it is written, For your sake, we are being killed all day long; we are regarded as sheep to be slaughtered. No, in all these things, we are more than conquerors through him who loved us. For I AM SURE that neither life, nor angels or rulers, nor things present or things to come, nor powers, nor height nor depth, nor ANYTHING ELSE in all creation, will be able to separate us from the love of God in Christ Jesus our Lord. (Romans 8:38-39. ESV). (Emphasis added)

The wonderful truth of this verse is that there is nothing that can separate us from the love of God. So, when a person decides to make this life changing decision, he or she has not removed themselves from the love of God.

However, I find that some believers tend to forget that. I recall a sad personal experience I had in a room full of pastors and ministers meeting for chaplaincy training for disaster relief. In that meeting, a pastor shared the story of a transgender woman who was attending church services in a local community. Some of the members of the church knew that she was transgender. The pastor welcomed her each Sunday and tried to make her feel at home. He, however, did not know that she was transgender.

After the pastor greeted her before the beginning of the service, a group came to him and told him that she was transgender. He took the information and did not appear to be alarmed by it. Other leaders in the group were offended. One Sunday, she came to the church, but the pastor was not there to greet her. He was away on vacation at the time. The woman was greeted by one of the leaders of the church. She asked for the pastor but was told he was out of town. She then asked the one who greeted her what she needed to do to join the church. This leader took it upon himself to tell her that there was no way that she could join the church unless she changed her lifestyle, meaning that she needed to change back to being a man. The woman was hurt and offended by that remark and left and never came back.

A discussion among the pastors and leaders then took place concerning this event. The comments made were disturbing at many levels. Throughout the discussion, jokes were made, and some even decided to mock this woman. One pastor spoke and made a point when he said, "She or her or it." Most of the men there laughed and continued to make fun of her. Others in the room, like myself, were offended by the way this woman was being mocked.

After a time of this kind of discussion, I finally spoke up and said, "Gentlemen, if we are going to agree with what this woman was told, then we need to take out most of our invitation songs, particularly the song that most churches sing during an invitation called *Just as I Am.* As a Christian, I have always been told, and I believe, that a person cannot do anything to make themselves worthy to become a Christian. There is only one thing that anyone can do to become a Christian, and that is to believe in Jesus as savior. When a person does that, then Jesus welcomes them into the kingdom. We send missionaries around the world to share that truth. Jesus loves you just as you are. You don't have to do anything to be loved by Him. He already loves you. So, for that leader to tell this woman she needed to transition back before she could be accepted was a complete contradiction of what we say we believe.

The Bible says that those who believe in Jesus become fishers of men. We then say, "We catch them, but He cleans them." Evidently, that does not include transgender men and women. After speaking up, others in the group shared the same opinion. After the meeting was over, the discussion continued, with some getting angry because of differing views. That was a sad day for me. I don't know or understand how someone can make those decisions, but it is not for me to understand or accept. It is for me to invite them to Christ and let them know that He will receive them.

As a continued note here, we just need to be reminded that Jesus loves these men and women who struggle with their identity. There is nothing they can do or decide to do that can separate them from the love of God. However, with children, it is different.

The Savage Abuse Of Children

When it comes to children, there should never be a decision to do any kind of transgender procedure. These young men and women do not have the mental or emotional capacity to make that kind of decision. There seems to be a lot of hysteria about transitioning children, and there is a great deal of effort to keep the desires of the student secret from his parents. Some parents indeed encourage transitioning their children, but it appears that most of the push is coming from those who have leadership positions in school or in government, and even some doctors in the medical profession rush to change a child's gender even before they reach puberty. Other, even more drastic procedures are being done, such as removing breasts from young girls and castrating young boys.

Teacher Wants To Hide Gender Information From Parents

One of the most egregious examples of gender hysteria comes from a Washington school teacher, Ms Knight, who formed an inappropriate relationship with a 5th-grade student who said that she wanted to be a boy. Knight determined that the best thing for the student was to hide this information from her parents. Knight began sending emails to the student telling her how to hide his gender questions and decisions from his parents. Emails were exchanged between the two and the Knight told the student to be sure and delete the emails so the parents would not know about what was happening. She told her that if her parents found out "they would out her."

In actuality, the teacher was following school policy regarding a student's privacy as well as the state's education policy regarding a student's privacy in medical matters. Knight then included other teachers in the school by sending all of those who had the student in class as to what was going on. She informed the other teachers that the student wanted to be called by her preferred pronoun of he/him/they/them, "which was his right." Knight told others who were involved in the coverup said schools need to keep information about children wanting to transition from "Christo-fascist parents." Knight felt she had the right to hide this information from parents because this was considered to be "classified health information."

Thankfully, the parents discovered what was going on and removed their daughter from the school. She is now identifying as a girl and is thriving. (brandikruse.locals.com, "How gender ideology led to a secret teacher-student relationship, July 12, 2023)

This is not just an anecdotal event. These kinds of events are quite common. It shows the contempt for parental authority over children, especially Christian parents. The Bible is very clear about who are the primary ones responsible for the education of children and it is the parent. The parents not only see that the child has an adequate secular education, but more than that, they have an ideology that wants their child to know their value to God. They also want their child to know that God made them who they are and has a plan for their life.

School Staff Steeped In Gender Indoctrination

Jon and Erin Lee found that the school their sixth-grade daughter attended was exposed to radical ideas about gender, sexuality, polyamory, and even suicide without the parent's knowledge or consent. Their daughter was told that the reason she was uncomfortable with her body was because she was transgender. A teacher invited their daughter to an after-school art club meeting, which in reality was to promote this godless gender ideology to a 5th-grade student without the knowledge of parents. The spreading of this ideology does nothing but confuse the child and cause emotional problems because they are being told that there is something wrong with them and the best way to fix it is through transitioning. (CBN.COM, School staff tries to turn daughter to be transgender, Steve Rees, August 16, 2024)

Colorado School Allows Boy To Share Bed With Girl On School Trip

Joes Wallace and his wife Serena sent their 11-year-old daughter on a school trip from Colorado to Washington, D.C. They were told by the school that boys would share rooms on one floor of the hotel and girls would share rooms on a different floor. Serena and her daughter were excited to go on the trip. The parents were horrified when their daughter called them in distress to tell them that she just found out her bedmate was a boy who identified as a girl. Turns out, this was all in line with school policy. A policy the school had failed to inform parents about. (Alliance Defending Freedom, "Colorado school district kept parents in the dark over Gender Identity rooming scheme," October 11, 2024).

School District Hides Information About Gender Transitioning Children.

The ideology concerning children and gender is reaching a critical time in America. Brutal and life-altering surgeries are being done on young children at an alarming rate. Stop the Harm is a group of medical professionals who monitor gender surgeries done on children. According to the data obtained, they learned that close to 14,000 children underwent some form of so-called sex-change procedures between 2019 and 2023. (CBN.com, US Hospitals Performed 14,000 Child-Sex Change Procedures From 2019 to 2023, Study Reveals. Tre'Goins-Phillips, October 11, 2024)

This Gender Savagery On Children Violates God's Love For Children

Matthew 18:10 **See that you do not despise one of these little ones. For I tell you that in heaven their angels always see the face of my Father who is in heaven**. Jesus considers children the weakest and the most vulnerable in society. This passage reveals the special care God provides for these little ones. According to this passage, these children have angels that watch over them. These angels not only guard over these children, but these angels always have God's attention. They always see his face. God is watching over the most vulnerable and takes very seriously the abuse of these little ones.

Psalm 127:3. **Behold children are a heritage from the Lord, the fruit of the womb a reward.** Every child is a gift from God. We are to look at our children as His gift. How, then, should we treat this gift? We tend to measure the value of gifts we receive by the ones who give them. How much greater is the value of any gift that comes from God? When we consider our children as God's gift, we will only do what is best for them. We will protect them from predators who wish to confuse them and cause them harm by teaching ideas they are not intellectually and emotionally ready to receive.

The second part of this verse is equally important. Our children are a gift from God, and they are a reward in the womb. Our children are a blessing, which indicates God's favor in our lives. His heart must be saddened to see how our nation has developed a culture where instead of children being a blessing and reward, they are considered by some to be an inconvenience and choose to abort the gift. How much more grief does He feel when we mutilate these children through gender savagery?

Luke 17:2. It would be better for him if a millstone would be hung around his neck and he were cast into the sea than that he should cause one of these little ones to sin.

In this passage, Jesus warns those who would lead children into sin. The judgment on them would Be severe. I think about the human trafficking of children, leading them into prostitution or sex slavery. I think about the gangs that recruit children into a violent life and encourage them to break the law. And I think about teachers, administrators, health officials, and government leaders who intentionally push transgender ideology on small children that makes them question who they are. These deceptive practices cause a lifetime of harm.

Chapter 11: The Savage Doctrine Of Critical Race Theory

One of the most savage ideologies to make its way into the mainstream is CRITICAL RACE THEORY. It is another of those godless theories that denies God's creation of all races. It is also a denial that God created all races as equals. Some races of people have indeed excelled over others, but that does not mean that one is superior to the other. This theory, as well as the transgender ideology, is being taught and promoted among young school-age children. Those who believe in CRT and transgenderism for children have the same kind of attitude. It is an attitude of aggression and intolerance. Those who teach and support CRT believe that they have the right and the obligation to help shape the minds of young children. And when parents push back and say they are opposed to this teaching, those parents are attacked.

CRT has a whole new way of looking at others. The teachings of CRT are rooted in Marxism. It is an ideology that diminishes another person because of their race, gender identity, and other characteristics. The Bible, on the other hand, teaches that every person has an intrinsic value that God places upon each person. When Jesus came to this earth to save men and women from their sins, he did not exclude any race or ethnic group of people. He came for all people.

When any person accepts Jesus as Lord and Savior, that person receives eternal life, a home in heaven, the presence of the Holy Spirit, forgiveness of sins, and redemption. Every person who comes to Jesus for salvation receives the same gifts and blessings that all other believers receive. When a person becomes a believer, he or she becomes a member of the body of Christ, which is the church. Every person in the church has the same standing. The one cross has saved all of us. We have been forgiven of our sins by the one who shed His blood. That person is Jesus. We all have the same presence of a home in heaven. It is only in Christ that every person stands on equal ground. It does not matter your social standing, your bank account, the kind of house you live in, or the car you drive. The only thing that matters is that each person puts their faith in Jesus and receives eternal life. All believers receive this eternal life. As we look at one of the definitions given to CRT, we can see just how different and contradictory it is to the Bible. britannia.Com defines CRT this way:" *critical race theory (CRT), intellectual and social movement and loosely organized framework of legal analysis based on the premise that race is not a natural, biologically grounded feature of physically distinct subgroups of human beings but a socially constructed (culturally invented) category that is used to oppress and exploit people of color. Critical race theorists hold that racism is inherent in the law and legal institutions of the United States insofar as they function to create and maintain social, economic, and political inequalities between whites and nonwhites, especially African Americans. Critical race theorists are generally dedicated to applying their understanding of the institutional or structural nature of racism to the concrete (if distant) goal of eliminating all race-based and other unjust hierarchies.* (Britannica.com, Social Sciences, Critical Race Theory, Updated, September 11, 2024)

The first thing we are told is that CRT is an intellectual and social movement with a loosely organized framework. So, from the beginning, we see that the definition is not totally agreed upon, which makes it even more confusing.

107

When reading the first sentence that describes it as an intellectual movement, my question is, "Whose intellect." What genius came up with this kind of concept. It evidently was not a Christian who believes what the Bible say about all people.

God says in His Word **My thoughts are not your thoughts, neither are your ways my ways, declares the Lord. So as the heavens are higher than the earth so are my ways higher than your ways and my thoughts higher than your thoughts. (Isaiah 55:8-9). (ESV).** The thinking of God is that all people, no matter their race or ethnicity, stand on level ground. They are all equal in their spiritual needs. They all need the salvation offered by the cross of Jesus. And then all Christians also stand equal before the cross. They all received the same salvation. They all are going to the same heaven and have the same savior. One is not greater than another. So, the intellect that created CRT did not come from the mind of God.

The beauty of the salvation that God provides is that it radically changes us. Accepting Jesus as a savior does not leave us the same. We are changed. We are changed in our attitudes toward others. CRT proposes that people cannot really change because of either their race or gender. For instance, a black individual will always be a victim of some kind. A white individual will always be a racist. CRT says that we just cannot help ourselves. We are what we are always going to be, and nothing can change that. A white person will always be a racist, and a black person will always be oppressed.

God's plan, on the other hand, does something that CRT can't do according to its own ideology. CRT can't change a person. It can only make him aware of what and who he is.

God, on the other hand, changes everything about a person. The Bible says that **any man in Christ is a new creature. OLD THINGS ARE PASSED AWAY, AND ALL THINGS BECOME NEW. (2 Corinthians 5:19). (ESV).** So, whatever a person was before he came to Christ, all that is changed. If he is racist, he then begins to love those who are different from he is. He sees people for their intrinsic worth to God and treats them as people of worth. He is not stuck in his attitudes or defined by social constructs or the writings of those who perpetuate racism with their theory. The Holy Spirit of God comes to live within Him and the love God has for others flows through him.

Do all self-identifying Christians live by the changes that God gave them? Of course not. But being a Christian means that we are never satisfied with where we are in our Christian life. We are always striving to be better and do better. We are always trying to become more like Christ in our life. We want to be better at loving others and seeing them for the person God made them. We want to look past the skin color and the ethnic life to see a person loved by God.

Those who hold to CRT believe that racism is inherent in the laws and in the institutions of America. Basically, America is a racist country, according to CRT. Are there racists in America? Yes. Are there those who are oppressed in certain places? Once again, the answer is yes. Does this, therefore, mean that the answer to these issues is CRT? In my opinion and in the opinion of others, ABSOLUTELY NOT.

The beginning of the church shows how God breaks down barriers between people of different races and ethnicities.

Acts 2:5 Now there were dwelling in Jerusalem Jews, devout men from every nation under heaven.

Act 2:6 And at this sound, the multitude came together, and they were bewildered because each one was hearing them speak in his own language.

Act 2:7 And they were amazed and astonished, saying, "Are not all these who are speaking Galileans?

Act 2:8 And how is it that we hear, each of us in his own native language?

Act 2:9 Parthians and Medes and Elamites and residents of Mesopotamia, Judea and Cappadocia, Pontus, and Asia.

Act 2:10 Phrygia and Pamphylia, Egypt and the parts of Libya belonging to Cyrene, and visitors from Rome.

Act 2:11 Both Jews and proselytes, Cretans and Arabians—we hear them telling in our own tongues the mighty works of God."

Act 2:12 And all were amazed and perplexed, saying to one another, "What does this mean?" (Act 2:5-10). (ESV)

This was the most remarkable day in the history of the church. After the resurrection of Jesus from the dead, He spent some time with His disciples, giving them some final words of instructions. The final thing he told them before he ascended into heaven was to "Go to Jerusalem and wait for the Holy Spirit to come." Their passage quoted above gives the results of that coming. This scripture says that there were people from all over the world there. The writer, Luke, goes on to list some of those countries. Verse 5 says that those who were there the day the Holy Spirit came were from every nation. These men and women came from all over the world.

The Bible says that something amazing happened. On that day, 3000 people became believers in Jesus. People from all over the world became believers in Jesus. Something else took place. Acts 2:44 says, **All those who believed were together and had all things in common. (KJV)**. The phrase being together means that they were united. They were spending time together praying, studying, and learning all they could about the person of Jesus. This was very important because, in a short time, these new disciples were going to be returning to their home countries, and they were going to be sharing the same message.

All these people from various nations were united. They were together. Let me share one other passage that demonstrates how God changes people in their relationship with one another.

Acts 8:26-38 says **Now an angel of the Lord said to Philip, "Rise and go toward the south to the road that goes down from Jerusalem to Gaza." This is a desert place.**

Act 8:27, And he rose and went. And there was an Ethiopian, a eunuch, a court official of Candace, queen of the Ethiopians, who was in charge of all her treasure. He had come to Jerusalem to worship

Act 8:28 and was returning, seated in his chariot, and he was reading the prophet Isaiah.

Act 8:29 And the Spirit said to Philip, "Go over and join this chariot."

Act 8:30 So Philip ran to him and heard him reading Isaiah the prophet and asked, "Do you understand what you are reading?"

Act 8:31 And he said, "How can I unless someone guides me?" And he invited Philip to come up and sit with him.

Act 8:32 Now, the passage of the Scripture that he was reading was this: "Like a sheep, he was led to the slaughter and like a lamb, before its shearer is silent, so he opens not his mouth.

Act 8:33 In his humiliation justice was denied him. Who can describe his generation? For his life is taken away from the earth."

Act 8:34 And the eunuch said to Philip, "About whom, I ask you, does the prophet say this, about himself or about someone else?"

Act 8:35 Then Philip opened his mouth, and beginning with this Scripture, he told him the good news about Jesus.

Act 8:36 And as they were going along the road, they came to some water, and the eunuch said, "See, here is water! What prevents me from being baptized?"

Act 8:38 And he commanded the chariot to stop, and they both went down into the water, Philip and the eunuch, and he baptized him. (Acts 8:26-38). (KJV)

In the second chapter of Acts, we saw that people from all over the world came together. Why did they come together? It was because of a person. That person was Jesus. Here, in the above passage, we are introduced to an Ethiopian who was an official in the queen's court. He was an important person in the politics of Ethiopia. Also, he was a black man. He was introduced to an interpretation of scripture from a Galilean. When this black man understood the message about the salvation of Jesus, he asked, "Is there any reason for me not to be baptized?" Phillip said no. His belief in Jesus as a savior was enough. So, this black man in the midst of a desert road received the same salvation that the hearers in Jerusalem received. A black man became a member of the church. He was a brother to all the other believers. The whole emphasis of being a member of the church of Jesus and a citizen of the kingdom of God is that we are united with people from all over the world.

I have had the privilege of going to various countries around the world. I met families in Honduras, Haiti, South Korea, and Brazil. I could not speak the language without an interpreter, but I knew them as my brothers and sisters in Christ. There was no issue of race. There was no issue of language or ethnicity. There was unity, and that unity was because of Jesus.

Critical Race Theory Is A Divisive Ideology

According to Tina Rameriz, who lives in Virginia and has a bi-racial daughter, "The school is teaching her daughter to make a determination on people based on color and external differences. For instance, it would teach my daughter that I am an oppressor by nature of my Hispanic-Caucasian heritage, despite the fact that I've defended human rights throughout my career. And that her father, who left her before she was born, is morally superior solely because of his race." She goes on to say, "Any parent can see how confusing this is for our children. But for a little girl who is being taught to hate the single parent who has loved and cared for her based on the color of her skin is absolutely repugnant and absurd. Worse still, this ideology would have my daughter hate and deny a part of herself. This must be stopped in our public schools." (Fox News, Critical race theory divides families - what this mom with a biracial child wants you to know. Tina Rameriz, March 26, 2021)

CRT is not the answer to the problems of racism we encounter. In my opinion, it is and has been the cause of increased division and hatred between people. The answer to the divisions we face is found in the only person who can bring us together, and that is Jesus.

Chapter 12: Christian Nationalism Is Not Christian

Over the past several years, we have been introduced to a new identification of Christian people. We're hearing the term "Christian Nationalism," and people are wondering, what does that mean? Some take this term to refer to Christians as patriots. They think it refers to those who love this country and are willing to do what is necessary to make our country great again. Most American feel that patriotism is a quality that every citizen must have. It is good for the citizens to love their country and be willing to do what is necessary to protect our freedoms and fight against any enemy that would seek to take away those freedoms. There is nothing wrong with being a patriot.

However, Christian Nationalism is far more than just the quality of patriotism. A patriot is someone who loves their country. Christian Nationalism is an attempt to define our country. It is the belief that the government should take steps to identify America as a Christian nation.

Scholars like Samuel Huntington have made the argument that America is defined by its "Anglo-Protestant" past and that we will lose our identity and our freedom if we do not preserve our cultural inheritance. (Christianity Today: What is Christian Nationalism, Paul D. Miller, February 3, 2021). In order to preserve our Christian culture in America, the government should put Christianity in a privileged position. A Christian Nationalist believes that Christianity and America are so interconnected that America can only be identified as a Christian Nation.

They point out that Christians were the only ones to establish the nation and win its freedom. There were no Muslim, Hindu, Buddhist, or other religions in the establishment of our nation. Therefore, since Christianity was the primary religious influence in the establishment of our country, Christian Nationalists believe Christianity should be the predominant and privileged religion. According to Andrew Whitehead, Christian Nationalists do not want a government for the people. Instead, they want a government for a particular people, particularly political and religious conservative white American Christians. (TIME MAGAZINE: Three threats Christian Nationalism poses to the United States, Andrew Whitehead, September 26, 2022)

Christian Nationalists believe that Christianity is the framework from which America was born. They believe that the framers of the Constitution thought that the best way for America to be a great nation was to be a Christian Nation.

A Christian Nationalist believes that all means necessary are to be used to restore America to its rightful place as a Christian Nation. According to some leaders, violence can be used when appropriate. This attitude was on display on January 6, 2022, when rioters attacked the capitol with the intention of keeping the election from being certified by the Senate.

Sadly, there were many Christian Nationalists in the crowd of rioters who stormed the capital on January 6, 2020. As the different news agencies panned the crowd and reported on the actions that were taken that day, people were holding signs that had Christian scripture and sayings on them. For instance, a sign that said JOHN 3:16 and JESUS SAVES were visible in that crowd as hundreds stormed the capital. Along with signs displaying scripture themes, others wore crusader-type shirts, indicating that they felt they were on the same kind of mission that the Crusaders of the ancient past were on. The crusaders of the past felt the need to deliver Jerusalem from the infidels. The current crusaders felt the need to deliver the capital of the U.S. from an immoral and corrupt government.

Some of those who stormed the capital on January 6 were attempting to force all Americans to embrace Christian nationalism. Their passion for wanting men and women to turn to God and accept Jesus Christ as savior is the passion of every believer. However, nowhere does Jesus commission His church and His disciples to force men and women to accept Christ as savior. He never forces people to believe in something they don't want to believe in. Jesus never forced people to follow Him.

The gospel of Matthew tells the story of a rich young man coming to Jesus to ask about eternal life. He wanted to know how to have eternal life. Jesus told him that in order to have eternal life, he must make God first in his life. The most important thing in this young man's life was his riches, his money. He just did not feel that he could walk away from that. The Bible says that after he heard what Jesus required, he became very sad because he was not able to turn loose of his riches. He walked away.

The young man was not the only one who was sad, but so was Jesus. Jesus was sad that this young man turned down the invitation to receive eternal life. He rejected the offer of eternal life. However, Jesus did not pursue this young man and try to force him to receive eternal life. He was sad at the choice this young man made, but he did not do anything to force the young man to change his mind.

And behold, a man came up to him, saying, "Teacher, what good deed must I do to have eternal life?"

And he said to him, "Why do you ask me about what is good? There is only one who is good. If you would enter life, keep the commandments."

He said to him, "Which ones?" And Jesus said, "You shall not murder, You shall not commit adultery, You shall not steal, You shall not bear false witness,

Honor your father and mother, and You shall love your neighbor as yourself."

The young man said to him, "All these I have kept. What do I still lack?"

Jesus said to him, "If you would be perfect, go, sell what you possess and give to the poor, and you will have treasure in heaven; and come, follow me."

When the young man heard this he went away sorrowful, for he had great possessions.

And Jesus said to his disciples, "Truly, I say to you, only with difficulty will a rich person enter the kingdom of heaven. (Matthew 19:16-220)

Even though the disciples and other followers thought that the Messiah was going to be a military and political Messiah. They believed that when the Messiah came, he would destroy the power of Rome over Israel, and this Messiah would establish a kingdom on earth, and Jerusalem would be the capital of this kingdom.

Yet, Jesus refused to accept that mission. His mission was not to bring an earthly kingdom but to bring a spiritual kingdom. His kingdom would not grow by force but through love and a personal invitation from Him to accept the salvation he had to offer. Jesus told Pilate at his trial, "**My kingdom is not of this world.**" (John 18:36)

According to Brad Onishi, "Christian Nationalism is based on the idea that America is a Christian Nation. He says that it is the belief that America was founded as a Christian nation and should be recognized as such. (PBS NEWS: What is Christian Nationalism and Why it Raises Concerns about Threats to Democracy, Laura Barron-Lopez and Sam Lane, Feb 1, 2024)

It is the belief that the federal government should declare that America is a Christian Nation. Ever since the arrival of Donald Trump on the political scene, there has been a marriage between evangelical Christians and the Republican Political party. Those who are Christian nationalists believe that it is the duty and the responsibility of those who are Christians to push for and support the work of those who wish to establish America as a Christian nation.

Sadly, those who promote this earthly nation do not understand the kingdom of God that is taught in the scripture. Those who are seeking to establish Christian nationalism in America have a distorted view of the gospel. They have a distorted view of the kingdom.

Some have advocated for an amendment to the Constitution. They want the new amendment to recognize and promote the Christian culture and history. With this Constitutional amendment, they want to reinstate prayer in our schools. They want American history to be taught in such a way that it shows the special kind of relationship that America has with God. These Christian Nationalists want children in school to understand that God created America with a special mission on earth, and that mission was to help the kingdom of God grow.

To recognize America's Christian heritage, others want to reinstitute prayer in public schools. Some work to enshrine a Christian nationalist interpretation of American history in school curricula, including that America has a special relationship with God or has been "chosen" by him to carry out a special mission on earth. Others advocate for immigration restrictions specifically to prevent a change to American religious and ethnic demographics or a change to American culture. Some want to empower the government to take stronger action to circumscribe immoral behavior. (CHRISTIANITY TODAY; Fred Miller, Feb 2, 2021)

The Many Questions That Arise Out Of Christian Nationalism

The first question is what form of Christianity will be used in forming this Nationalistic government. Will it be Baptist, Methodist, Catholic, Pentecostal, or Evangelicalism? Each of these Christian belief systems has different policies in which their church and their denominations are run. For Baptists, each church is independent from all other churches. Methodists have a denomination that a General Conference, a Council of Bishops, and a Judicial Counsel govern. The Catholic Church is governed by a Pope, a Council of Cardinals, Bishops, and priests. All Christian organizations have different organizational structures. The question then is which one of those will be the dominant one to help govern this National Christian government.

Christian Nationalists fail to recognize that Jesus came to establish a spiritual kingdom, not a physical one. The kingdom of God does not have geographical boundaries. Neither does it have a dominant ethnic group as a majority.

The kingdom of God is made up of men and women from all nations and all ethnic groups.

Some have suggested that Christian Nationalists have within their movement those who support and believe in White Supremacy. This is in complete opposition to the word of God. The Bible is very clear that God is no respecter of persons based on their race, language, ethnicity, or the color of their skin.

In Galatians 3:28, Paul said, **There is neither Jew nor Gentile, neither slave nor free, nor is there male and female, for you are all one in Christ Jesus**. There is no superior race of people in the kingdom of God. No group has more spiritual authority than any other group.

In the kingdom of God, there are no geographical policies or national boundaries. There are no borders. Jesus taught that the Holy Spirit empowers the kingdom of God. He also described the Holy Spirit as the wind. You can feel it, but you can't see it, and you don't know where it comes from.

Jesus said in John 3:7-8 **Do not marvel that I said to you, 'You must be born again. The wind blows where it wishes, and you hear its sound, but you do not know where it comes from or where it goes. So, it is with everyone who is born of the Spirit.** Notice how he describes the Spirit as wind. He does this because he wants us to know that the Spirit of God has unlimited power and authority as to our salvation. The Holy Spirit goes anywhere and uses His authority and influence to help bring men and women into the kingdom.

Christian Nationalism Is Not Describing The Kingdom Of God.

Christian Nationalism is attempting to create an anomaly in the kingdom of God. The way to change government is not through a government takeover of any kind. It is through the sharing of the gospel with those who do not know Jesus as savior. It is through Christian men and women living out their faith in the real world. It shows the love of Jesus to men and women of every race, color, and creed. It is treating men and women with respect and dignity. In the kingdom of God, there is no anti-semitism. There is no racism. Abuse of any kind does not exist in the kingdom of God.

It is true that even though the kingdom of God is present in the hearts and lives of believers, we do not have it all down perfectly. We are still sinners who have been saved by grace. When we sin, we confess our sins, repent, and ask God to give us a new start. So, instead of seeking to change government through a political movement, let us follow the guide Jesus left us. Let us change our nation by living our faith in front of others. Let us change our nation by living in a way that honors Him. Let us change our nation by lifting up **Jesus, who said If I be lifted up, I will draw all men to me. (John 12:32, KJV).**

Chapter 13: Good News In Scandalous Times

Throughout the book, we have been talking about issues that are tearing apart the fabric of our society. We talked about things that affect our children, our families, our marriages, and other matters that are not just controversial but are very destructive. As we've talked about each of these particular problems, we looked at some of the solutions that have been offered and found that no solution has been found to fix our problems. Whatever solutions we come up with only seem to make matters worse, not better. Our proposed solutions to the controversies that we face simply reveal how helpless we are in solving the things that are tearing us apart. We discovered that we are absolutely helpless to solve these problems that are plaguing our country today. The only real solutions come from our dependence and our obedience to the word of God.

The good news is found in all the promises of God. Yes, these are savage times, but we serve a God who promises that these times will end. He will eventually bring these times to a close. But until He does, He will continue to reign over all things. He will continue to accomplish His purpose, and nothing will prevent Him.

Most of all, He will be with us through all these times to guide us, strengthen us, and be present in us until He ushers in the fullness of His kingdom where there will be;

No more danger to the unborn

No more questions or confusion over gender

No more racism

No more political unrest

No more disobedience to His Authority

No more war, only perfect peace

No more crime

Until that day comes, the Lord provides us with the tools to live in these times. Throughout history, there have been enemies of the church who sought to destroy it and wipe it from the face of the earth. However, in each of those hard times, the Lord has protected His church. He promised that there was nothing on earth or even in hell that could destroy His church because it was built upon the rock; He is the rock.

The apostle Paul reveals the kind of weapons and tools God gives us to navigate these savage times.

He gives us His spiritual armor to help us defend ourselves and, at the same time, be aggressive in sharing the gospel. Paul describes the armor in Ephesians 6.

Eph 6:10 Finally, be strong in the Lord and in the strength of his might.

Eph 6:11 Put on the whole armor of God, that you may be able to stand against the schemes of the devil.

Eph 6:12 For we do not wrestle against flesh and blood, but against the rulers, against the authorities, against the cosmic powers over this present darkness, against the spiritual forces of evil in the heavenly places.

Eph 6:13 Therefore take up the whole armor of God, that you may be able to withstand in the evil day, and having done all, to stand firm.

Eph 6:14 Stand, therefore, having fastened on the belt of truth, and having put on the breastplate of righteousness,

Eph 6:15 and, as shoes for your feet, having put on the readiness given by the gospel of peace.

Eph 6:16 In all circumstances take up the shield of faith, with which you can extinguish all the flaming darts of the evil one;

Eph 6:17 and take the helmet of salvation, and the sword of the Spirit, which is the word of God,

Eph 6:18 praying at all times in the Spirit, with all prayer and supplication. To that end, keep alert with all perseverance, making supplication for all the saints,

Eph 6:19 and also for me, that words may be given to me in opening my mouth boldly to proclaim the mystery of the gospel,

Eph 6:20 for which I am an ambassador in chains, that I may declare it boldly, as I ought to speak. (ESV)

Not only does He give us the ability to live and prosper in these times, but He reminds us of a greater day coming.

In the closing pages of Revelation, Jesus tells us what we have to look forward to.

Rev 21:1 Then I saw a new heaven and a new earth, for the first heaven and the first earth had passed away, and the sea was no more.

Rev 21:2 And I saw the holy city, new Jerusalem, coming down out of heaven from God, prepared as a bride adorned for her husband.

Rev 21:3 And I heard a loud voice from the throne saying, "Behold, the dwelling place of God is with man. He will dwell with them, and they will be his people, and God himself will be with them as their God.

Rev 21:4 He will wipe away every tear from their eyes, and death shall be no more, neither shall there be mourning, nor crying, nor pain anymore, for the former things have passed away."

Rev 21:5 And he who was seated on the throne said, "Behold, I am making all things new." Also, he said, "Write this down, for these words are trustworthy and true."

We could go on and on. The main thing is that's going to be a great day and **WHAT A DAY THAT WILL BE.**

Bibliography

(FOREST GUMP; THE MOVIE, Released 1994)

(AVATAR; THE MOVIE, Released December 10, 2009)

(W.F. Adeney, The Pulpit Commentary Gospel of Matthew, Copyright © 2001, 2003, 2005, 2006, 2010 by Biblesoft, Inc.)

(BiblicalHermeneuticsstackexchange.com, 2024)

The DNC Hellish Abortion Rituals; The celebration of Death, The real agenda, Lila Rose, Fox News Digital, MSN.com*)*

(The Houston Herald; Thousands of churches are closing every year," by the Herald Staff, January 26, 2023)

(The New York Post; Public Schools are teaching our children to hate America," Mary Kay Linge, February 22, 2020)

(The balladofAmerica.org; America the Beautiful; About the Song.)

(Jonathan Turley, The Greatest Single threat to America is hiding in plane sight", Fox News Opinion, October 23, 2023).

(SALON: Eli Mystal, Our Constitution is trash, but the Supreme Court can be fixed," by Dean Obeidallah, March 23, 2022)

(HARVARD LAW SCHOOL FACULTY BIOGRAPHY: The Constitution is Broken and does not need to be reclaimed," Ryan D. Doerfler of Harvard and Samuel Moyn, August 19, 2022)

(FEDERAL NEWS NETWORK, Jeffery Neal, January 4, 2021)

(The Christian Post; Bernie Sanders thinks all Christians are disqualified from Public office." Julie Roys, July 8, 2017).

(THE FEDERALIST: Under Tim Walz, Minnesota Banned Christians From Teaching In Public Schools" Joy Pullan, August 27, 2024)

(Fox News Media, Aubrey Spady, August 24, 2024)

(TORONTO SUN:" High School student suspended and arrested for saying there are only two genders," Brian Lilly, February 8, 2023).

(FOX NEWS: Vermont encourages everyone to replace "sons and daughters" with gender-neutral terms in school."Aubrey Spady, August 29, 2024)

(FOX NEWS: Washington teacher says schools must do more to keep student info from Christo-fascist parents, Joshua Nelson, February 28, 2023)

(The Christian Post: Nearly 70% of Born Again Christians believe that other religions can lead to heaven, Senior Reporter; Leonardo Blair, October 21, 2021)

(NewsBreak.com; THE INDEPENDENT: Christian teacher sacked for online post saying She is not alone. Callum Parke, October 2, 2024)

(FOXNEWS.COM; Man fined for standing silently across from an abortion clinic, and the officers could not tell him what his crime was. Writer Kendal Tietz, May 25, 2024)

(FOXNEWS.COM. *Collage fires theologian for his tweet against homosexuality: Jon Brown (Fox News Reporter) March 19, 2023)*

(CBSNEWS.COM, *Man accused of yelling at priest and calling him the devil, Shirley Bortz, April 25, 2024)*

(INDY100.COM, *Abortion activists strip down during Joel Olsteen sermon, Brianna Robinson June 7, 2022)*

(brandikruse.locals.com, "How gender ideology led to a secret teacher-student relationship, July 12, 2023)

(CBN.COM, School staff tries to turn daughter to be transgender, Steve Rees, August 16, 2024)

(Alliance Defending Freedom, "Colorado school district kept parents in the dark over Gender Identity rooming scheme," October 11, 2024).

(Britannica.com, Social Sciences, Critical Race Theory, Updated, September 11, 2024)

(Fox News, Critical race theory divides families - what this mom with a biracial child wants you to know. Tina Rameriz, March 26, 2021)

(Christianity Today: What is Christian Nationalism, Paul D. Miller, February 3, 2021).

(TIME MAGAZINE: Three threats Christian Nationalism poses to the United States, Andrew Whitehead, September 26, 2022)

(PBS NEWS: What is Christian Nationalism and why it raises concerns about threats to Democracy, Laura Barron-Lopez and Sam Lane, Feb 1, 2024)

(CHRISTIANITY TODAY; Fred Miller, Feb 2, 2021)

9 781967 668045